SERBO-CROATIAN READER

An anthology of extracts from the works of contemporary
Serbo-Croatian writers, with translations and notes.

This book contains a wide variety of short extracts (thirty
in all) from works by modern Serbo-Croatian writers. The
majority are of a fictional nature, and each item has a certain
completeness in itself. The purpose of the book is not only to
make these works accessible to English-speaking readers but
also to aid students of Serbo-Croat. Attention has therefore
been given, in most of the translations, to presenting render-
ings that are as literal as possible. These are supplemented
by the Notes.

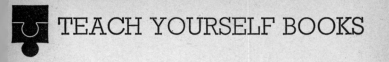

TEACH YOURSELF BOOKS

SERBO-CROATIAN
READER

Vera Javarek

B.A., Ph.D.

*Former Lecturer in
Serbo-Croatian Language and Literature
in the University of London*

ST. PAUL'S HOUSE WARWICK LANE
LONDON EC4P 4AH

First published 1974

ISBN 0 340 05384 4

Printed and bound in Great Britain
for The English Universities Press, Ltd.,
by Richard Clay (The Chaucer Press), Ltd., Bungay, Suffolk

Contents

Part III   NOTES AND BIBLIOGRAPHY

To
NICHOLAS

Preface

All the literary passages in this book have been taken from the works of prominent Yugoslav writers of our time. They have been chosen with the needs of the student of the language principally in mind, but it is hoped that their literary value also will be appreciated. I regret that they are so short, and especially that only the briefest of short stories could be given in their full form, but in order that the book should serve its practical purpose it had to include as many items and as much variety as possible in a limited space. The context of a few of the extracts is explained in the Notes; but I think the passages from novels and short stories will be found, on the whole, to have a certain completeness in themselves. If the reader is tempted to turn to any of the works from which these passages have been selected (see the Bibliography), this book will more than have served its purpose.

In order to do justice to the authors whose works are represented in this book freer translations, in more natural English, would often have been preferable to those I have given; but these would have presented problems to students of the language. The arrangement is from the easier to the more difficult texts, and the later items are translated less literally than the earlier ones; but throughout the book, where phrases or sentences could not be given literal translations in reasonably normal English, their construction is clarified in the Notes.

If you are reading this book with the help of the Notes you are advised to work through it from the beginning, as the explanations of exceptional or less usual word forms, and references to the Grammar *Teach Yourself Serbo-Croat*, are not usually repeated.

It is a great pleasure to record my grateful thanks to the Yugoslav writers who so kindly gave me permission to use their works for this book: to Ivo Andrić, Tvrtko Čubelić, Antonije Isaković, Radomir Konstantinović, Miroslav Krleža, Mihailo Lalić, Ranko Marinković, Slobodan Novak, Meša Selimović, Ivan Slamnig, Petar Šegedin, Antun Šoljan, Nikola Šop, Dragutin Tadijanović and Aleksandar Vučo; and to Uroš Desnica in respect of the work of Vladan Desnica, whose death in 1967 meant a great loss to Yugoslav letters. I would also like to express my warm thanks to Nebojša Tomašević, editor of *Revija* (*Review*), for his kindness in sending me the original Serbo-Croatian versions of articles which had appeared in the English editions of his magazine; and to Vladeta Janković and Dejan Petrović for their generous help in the planning and preparation of this book.

Vera Javarek
London, June 1973

Part I

SERBO-CROATIAN TEXTS

1   *Strah u željeznici*

DRAGUTIN TADIJANOVIĆ

U desetoj svojoj godini, u svibnju 1915, prvi put sam se vozio željeznicom, iz Broda do Vrpolja. Moja mati i baka povedoše i mene: išli smo u posjet mom ocu, u Đakovo. U ono vrijeme, nekoliko mjeseci, bio je on *purš*, posilni, vojnog liječnika koji se zvao, ako se dobro sjećam, Tallian, iz Osijeka. Sobom su ponijele i košaru jagoda, poklon tome liječniku.

Kao da mí je, i sada, u kostima strah koji sam pretrpio dok nije kondukter pregledao putne karte. Prije njegova dolaska mati mi je govorila:

— Zguri se. Zguri se da ne budeš tako velik.

— Kako ću se zguriti? Ne znam ja to — odgovorih namršteno.

Baka doda:

— Poslušaj svoju mater. Zar ti je teško zguriti se?

Ja sam naime, za svoju dob, jače bio razvijen, bojale su se da će i za me morati da plate čitavu kartu a ne polovicu kao za djecu ispod deset godina. A ja sam i imao polovicu karte koju sam pažljivo držao u ruci.

Kad je kondukter ušao u vagon, prvi koga je ugledao bio sam ja. Počeo sam drhtati, od straha. On mi reče:

— Digni se, mali. Da vidim koliki si!

Pokušavajući da što više uvučem ramena, ustadoh, zguren, i priđoh majci, uplašen.

— Je li to tvoj sin? — zapita on majku.

Odgovori brže baka:

— Da, gospodine. A moj je unuk.

— Ima li kartu?

— Kako ne bi imao.

— Da vidim.

I ja, bojažljivo, pružih kondukteru svoju polovicu karte. A on će majci i baki:

— Mislite li vas dvije da ja ne vidim? Stariji je on od deset godina!

— Ma nije, gospodine, nije — povikaše one uglas.

— Kako nije? Vidite koliki je. Nemojte vi meni govoriti. Imam ja dobro oko.

Drhtao sam kao šiba na vodi. Mati još jednom odgovori:

— Nije, gospodine, nema. Imat će deset godina o Sisvetima. Tako se rodio.

— Vidim ja dobro, i predobro.

Kondukter ponovo svrne pogled na me; umirao sam od straha, samo što nisam zaplakao.

— Dajte vaše karte! — zapovjedi strogo. Pa ih brzo probuši. Priđe k meni i rukom mi malo potrese rame:

— Ne boj se, junače! Hajde, hajde, nek te voda nosi.

Okrene se drugim putnicima, a baka me stade tješiti i hrabriti da i on čuje:

— Neće tebi gospodin ništa. Vidiš da je dobar.

Iz mojih očiju kanuše suze — od njegove dobrote.

2   Iz priče *Nas troje*

DRAGUTIN TADIJANOVIĆ

Ne očekujući da će itko pristupiti u moju blizinu, sjedoh na uzvišicu kraj uzglavlja Vojnovićeva groba, uz čempres; izvadio sam notes i prekriživši nogu preko noge napisao prvih pet stihova. Osnovna misao, koju sam kanio izraziti u pjesmi, nije mi bila potpuno jasna. Dizao sam glavu iznad papira, pogledavao uokolo.

Najednom se preda mnom stvorio onaj dječak.

Nisam ga očekivao, nikako.

Zaklopim notes i među nama dvojicom ponovo se započne razgovor:

— Znaš li ti tko leži u ovom grobu?

— Rekli su mi: nekakav pjesnik.

— Kako se zove?

— Ne znam.

— Pročitaj mu ime. Znaš i sâm čitati.

— *Ovdje počiva pjesnik Ivo Vojnović 1857–1929.*

— Ako budeš polazio škole, nauke, o njemu ćeš mnogo čuti.

— Gledajte! Na onom je grobu slika jednog dječaka!

— Znam. Vidio sam je.

Moj mali subesjednik priđe k susjednom grobu, do zida, i zagleda se izbliza u sliku mrtvoga dječaka. Polako stane čitati riječi uklesane ispod slike: *Ne zaboravi nas, Milo.*

Još glasnije reče:

— Milo se zvao sin moje tetke.

— Jesi li ga poznavao?

— Nisam.

— Kako mu je prezime?

— Stanković.

— Na tom grobu piše: Stanković.

— Pa da. Pa to je sin moje tetke, Milo. On je poginuo!

— Poginuo? Kada?

— U ratu. Kod bombardiranja. On je išao, on je držao ruke na tjemenu, a jedan je avion bacio bombu, i krhotina ga je pogodila u glavu, i sve je bilo krvavo, i ruke. Imao je dvanaest godina.

— Zar nisi znao da je ovdje pokopan?

— Nisam. Sad vidim. Pa to je Milo.

Ponovo se približio dječakovoj slici i stao je pažljivo razgledavati:

— Ima bijelu kapu na glavi.

— Da! — rekoh glasno, a pomislih: Kao da je slutio da je smrt za se odabrala upravo to mjesto na njegovu tijelu da ga sa zemljom sravni.

Nas dvojica ne progovorismo više ni riječi.

3 Iz priče *Šimo Šimić*

DRAGUTIN TADIJANOVIĆ

Govorit ću, kako obećah, o Šimi Šimiću.

Jedne subote, bilo je to u prosincu 1917, vratio se moj djed, u kasnu noć, s kolima, iz Sijekovca.

Dočekaše ga, kao uvijek, baka i moja mati.

Ali djed nije bio sâm. S njim je bio dječak od nekih petnaest godina, u poderanom odijelu, s krpama na nogama, gologlav, mršav, prozebao. Kašljao je, ne, hripao je od kašlja.

— A ko ti je taj? — upitat će baka.

— Čuvat će nam krave. Znaš i sama da nemamo govedara.

Dok su baka i mati rasprezale konje, uđoše njih dvojica, djed i nepoznati dječak, u toplu sobu. Kad je djed odvrnuo fitilj petrolejke, jače je zasjalo, i ja sam, iz kreveta, ugledao tog dječaka koji je od zime drhtao kao da ga sedam groznica trese. Bio je on koju godinu stariji od mene, viši od mene, ali meni se tada pričinilo kao da mu nema više nego jedanaest, dvanaest godina, i pomislio sam: ovo je bijeda, nevolja, o kojoj sam dosad samo slušao. Uhvatio sam brzi njegov pogled, malo preplašen, kojim je osmotrio sobu, i mene, i zaustavio ga najposlije na velikom domaćem kruhu, na stolu pripremljenom za djedovu večeru.

Ja nisam skidao oka s toga dječaka dok su god njih dvojica, djed i on, večerali a djed ga nutkao:

— Uzmi, uzmi još!

Mislio sam: gdje će on spavati?

Kad je večera bila dogotovljena, djed ga zovne:

— Hajde ti sada sa mnom, pokazat ću ti gdje ćeš noćivati.

I oni iziđoše. Pomislih: da sam ja na njegovu mjestu, kako li bi me bilo strah.

Dugo, dugo nisam mogao zaspati.

On je spavao na štaglju. U sijenu. U mrklome mraku.

Ujutro, kad sam se probudio, bio je već u sobi, obučen u toplije odijelo, obuven u opanke, zažaren u licu.

Gledao je kroz prozor, u selo. Mene nije htio da vidi.

Obojica smo šutjeli.

Bio bih volio da me išta zapita. Ali držao se kao da mene i nema.

Čulo se samo kucanje sata s dugim tankim lancima, na zidu kraj drugoga prozora, onoga gdje je, noću, spavala baka.

Prekinuo sam šutnju, uzbuđen, i upitao ga gotovo šapatom:

— Čuj me! Kako se zoveš?

— Šta te briga! — odgovori on glasnije, ne okrenuvši se.

— Pitam te. Volio bih znati kako ti je ime?

— Šimo.

— A kako još? Prezime!

— Šimić.

— Odakle si?

— Neću ti kazati! — naglo se okrene i pogleda me.

Ako se ne varam, oči su mu bile pune suza. Rekoh mu:

— I ne moraš, Šimo. Znat ću ja to od moga dide.

— Pa znaj!

Ponovo nastade šutnja, dok nije u sobu ušla mati i zovnula me:

— Ustani, već je kasno. Sunce je izašlo davno.

I tako, šta da pripovijedam kako je bilo iz dana u dan, čitavu zimu, do proljeća.

Ja sam pješačio u Brod, u školu, a Šimo je čuvao krave. Od djeda je dobio gunjac i kožnu torbu s kaišem preko ramena koju bi mu baka napunila kruhom, slaninom, sirom, lukom, već kako koji dan.

Čim bi okopnio snijeg, tjerao je krave u Dolove, u Pribudovac, i podveče se s njima vraćao kući. Nitko ga nije čuo da bi ikad zapjevao kao ostali govedari. Posvršavao bi večernje poslove, u štali, u dvorištu, pa večerao, pa se popeo na štagalj i zaspao.

A možda i ne bi zaspao nego dugo gledao otvorenim očima u mrak?

Nikome nije htio reći ima li oca, majku, brata, sestru? Gdje su? Kako žive?

Djed ga je moj našao bio u Sijekovcu, sama, promrzla, gladna, dovezao ga kući, nahranio, obukao, i sad on, Šimo Šimić, razmišlja, dugo razmišlja, kako bi se domogao svoga doma, negdje daleko, preko Save, tamo gdje se rodio i odrastao među svojima.

Granulo je proljeće; jaglaci su probili iz trave.

Šimo Šimić prvi put je pošao za kravama na Sječe, na Marića brdo, odakle je vidio Savu i Brod, kroz koji se one noći provezao s mojim djedom; ugledao je, u daljini, svoju Bosnu.

Čiji je čuo glas da ga doziva?

Kad je već pala duboka noć, krave se još ne vratiše.

— Da nije on možda uteko? — netko kaza od mojih.

Da. Nikad nam se nije više vratio.

Sjećao sam ga se dugo, Šime Šimića. Pa vidite, i danas.

4   Narodna pripovijetka *Lav i čovjek*

iz zbirke TVRTKA ČUBELIĆA

Stara lavica othranila je nasred pustinje mladoga lava i ulila mu u grudi mržnju na čovjeka koji mu je ubio oca i dva brata.

Kad je mladi lav odrastao i osjetio da mu je snaga golema, oprosti se s majkom obećavši da tako dugo neće imati mira dok ne nađe i ne uništi svoga najvećeg neprijatelja — čovjeka.

Dugo je putovao neprestano tražeći ono za čim je pošao. Na pučini pješčanog mora susretne jednom veliku životinju s dugim savijenim vratom, obraslu mrkom dlakom, a s dvije grbe na leđima. Odmah je srdito zapita:

— Ti si čovjek, je li?

Deva uzdahne i mirno mu odgovori:

— Ne! Čovjek drukčije izgleda. Ti držiš da sam ja snažan stvor. I jesam, nitko ne može tako dugo podnositi glad i žeđu kao ja. Nitko me ne može stići kad se požurim po ovoj pješčanoj pustinji. A ja sam ipak čovječji rob. Ja pred njim kleknem kad on hoće da me uzjaše; on upravlja svom mojom snagom na svoju korist, a zato mi dopušta da se mogu hraniti bodljikavim biljkama. Poslije pak moje smrti čovjek mi odere kožu da od nje napravi sebi šator da se zakloni od vrućeg sunca i od zla vremena. Ne, ja nisam čovjek.

Lavić se zamisli pa ode dalje. Sad naiđe na neku čudnovatu životinju. Na čelu je imala dva roga. Vrat joj je bio debeo i jak. Kad joj se lav približi, ona snažno lupi nogom o zemlju. To će biti čovjek — pomisli lav pa odmah zapita:

— Jesi li ti čovjek?

— Ja čovjek? Ljuto se varaš, dragi moj. Ja sam sluga njegov, a on gospodar nad svima nama. Natakne mi jaram na vrat pa moram orati i najveće terete vući. Meso mi pojede, a od kože pravi sebi opanke.

Lav se namršti pa ode dalje.

Idući tako začuje neki topot: zemlja se kao potresla, i evo dotrča stasita plemenita životinja. Odskače joj duga griva na vratu, a straga joj se previja dugi rep.

— Ha, ti si čovjek! — reče lav.

Konj ržući zastane i tužno odgovori:

— Nisam, ja sam sluga čovjekov.

— Zar ti njegov sluga?! A gle kako si jak i ponosit!

— Takav sam kad sam sâm. Ali kad sam u blizini čovjeka, onda mi se ponos pokunji. On mi turi žvale u usta, zauzda me pa me uzjaše, a ja ga moram nositi kudgod je njemu drago. U čovjeka je moć, i mi smo svi ništa prema njemu.

Sad se lav odšulja u šumu. Čuo je neke udarce kao da netko cijepa drva. Približi se da vidi šta je. Tu vidi neki omanji, prema sebi neznatni stvor. Sad je baš oborio gorostasnu jelu, samo je ostao još donji dio stabla, panj, dva pedlja visok nad zemljom. Lav zapita toga neznanca je li gdje vidio čovjeka.

— Ti čovjeka tražiš? — odgovori čovjek. — Što bi s njime?

— Ubio mi oca i dva brata, hoću mu se osvetiti.

— Pa to je dobro, zaista dobro. Alah neka ti pomogne!

Lavu je ta pohvala godila. On ispriča sve što je čuo o svome ocu i svojoj braći. Još zamoli čovjeka neka samo nastavi svoj rad.

Čovjek je baš zasjekao panj pa zamoli lava da mu pomogne. Lav upita kako će mu pomoći.

— Nemam klina da ga metnem u ovaj rascjep. Budi dobar pa turi svoju nogu unutra.

— Hoću, drage volje.

Čim lav turi nogu u rascjep, čovjek izvuče sjekiru, a lavu se noga ukliješti u pukotini. Lav je bio uhvaćen.

Tada mu tek čovjek reče da je on čovjek.

— Vidim ja šta je — uzdahne lav. — Da je to po snazi, ti ne bi bio tako strašan, ali to čini tvoja vještina. A sad ćeš me ubiti, je li?

— Neću, pustit ću te da odeš i da pričaš kako je čovjekova vještina jača od najjačih sila. Ali on katkada ima i milostivo srce. Jer inače ne bi bio — čovjek.

5 Iz članka *I Trebnje je rođeno*

iz časopisa *Revija*

Malo slovenačko mesto Trebnje, na pola puta između Zagreba i Ljubljane, sa jedva stotinu kuća, smešteno u najsiromašnijoj opštini Slovenije, postalo je važan centar okupljanja jugoslovenskih naivnih slikara. Prvi susret predstavljao je deset uzbudljivih dana za te slikare, koji se dotle nisu poznavali među sobom a možda ni čuli jedni za druge. Učestvovalo je celo stanovništvo. Svakog dana građani su dolazili da gledaju kako njihovi gosti rade na staklu, platnu i drvetu. Na kraju su radovi postavljeni pored zida, jer pogodne prostorije za izložbu nije bilo.

Slikari su za uzvrat za gostoprimstvo i troškove puta morali da naslikaju po jednu sliku i ostave Trebnju. Od slika koje su ostavili formirana je stalna galerija. Sada Trebnje pored godišnjeg salona koji otvaraju najvažnije jugoslovenske ličnosti ima lepo uređenu stalnu galeriju i četiri samostalne izložbe godišnje: dve iz Slovenije a dve iz drugih republika.

6 Iz članka *Planinski turizam*

iz časopisa *Revija*

Turiste najviše privlače obale toplog Jadranskog mora. Velika razuđenost jugoslovenske morske obale stvorila je čitav niz većih i manjih zaliva sa poluostrvima i rtovima, sa ostrvima i uvalama, pitomim dragama i peskovitim plažama. Duž čitave obale, čija dužina iznosi preko dve hiljade kilometara, ređa se više od hiljadu manjih i većih ostrva. Zato su Jugoslaviju i nazvali ,,zemljom sa hiljadu ostrva".

Ali pored mora Jugoslavija ima i lepe planinske predele. Od alpskog gorja na krajnjem severozapadu do živopisnih jezera i rečnih dolina na makedonskom jugu, kontinentalni deo je takođe pun raznovrsnih pejzaža. Međutim, nedostupnost nekim najlepšim planinskim predelima u Jugoslaviji i nedostatak hotela u tim oblastima, uticalo je da su one ostale neotkrivene za turiste. Tek poslednjih godina, sa izgradnjom sve više modernih autoputeva i saobraćajnica i podizanjem hotela, polako se otvaraju vrata na planinskim prostranstvima.

7 Iz članka *Pakao u dolini raja*

iz časopisa *Revija*

Dolina reke Soče u Sloveniji je jedna od najlepših u Jugoslaviji. Putovati uz Soču predstavlja doživljaj koji se lako ne zaboravlja.

Nedaleko od Tolmina, lepog gradića u dolini Soče, gore visoko u planini, onde gde može stupiti noga samo iskusnog planinara, ugnezdilo se seoce Čadrg.

Jedna legenda priča da se za vreme svog izgnanstva iz Firence veliki italijanski pesnik Dante zaustavio na duže vreme u Čadrgu, Tolminu i okolini. Ovaj ga je kraj toliko impresionirao da je svakog dana dolazio pred jednu privlačno smeštenu pećinu iznad rečice Zalaščice, koja stotinu metara duboko dole vijuga ponorom veličanstvenog klanca. Dante bi, kako kaže legenda, sedeo na kamenu pred pećinom, u crvenom ogrtaču i s kapom iste boje na glavi. Uvek je nešto pisao, a predveče se spuštao vijugavim kozjim i vučjim stazicama kroz kameno bespuće prema Tolminu. Legenda čak priča da je Dante, inspirisan jedinstvenim pejzažima i divljom lepotom stravičnih kanjona, napisao svoje najveličanstvenije delo, *Božansku komediju.*

8 Iz članka *Dugo putovanje sedog pesnika*

iz časopisa *Revija*

Jedne hladne zimske noći 1942. godine, 66-godišnji pesnik Vladimir Nazor, zajedno sa svojim mladim prijateljem — pesnikom Ivanom Goranom Kovačićem, autorom potresne poeme *Jama*—krenuo i najzad dospeo u Narodno-oslobodilačku vojsku.

Pesnik je i ovde progovorio sa fronta. On je bio ohrabrenje ljudima u mučnom nevremenu. Voleli su ga i čuvali. I glavni komandant, maršal Tito, izdao je precizna uputstva da se starom pesniku olakša, koliko je moguće, partizanski život.

. . . . . .

Posle proboja obruča u najtežoj petoj ofanzivi, onda kada su bile gladne i iscrpljene partizanske jedinice opkoljene od višestruko nadmoćnog neprijatelja, Vrhovni štab se nalazio na brdu blizu jednog bosanskog sela iz koga su stanovnici pobegli u šumu strahujući od surove odmazde Nemaca. Vladimir Nazor bio je toliko iznemogao da su ga nosili. Ali i tada, i u mnogim drugim teškim časovima, on je bio spreman za šalu.

Blizu, u jednoj kolibi, nalazio se Vladimir Zečević, koji je bio sveštenik pre nego što je prihvatio pušku. Partizani su ga zvali Pop-Vlado.

Čuvši da se među partizanima nalazi i jedan pop, nekoliko starica nabere korpu jagoda i krenu popu da im oprosti grehe i da ih blagoslovi, jer svakog se časa moglo poginuti. Umesto Pop-Vlade, starice su naišle na Vladu Nazora, koji je takođe imao bradu.

— Blagoslovi, oče! — i starice zauzeše pobožnu pozu.

— Da ste blagoslovene! — uzviknu spremno pesnik, — što se mene tiče. Jagode ostavite ovdje. Pravi blagoslov potražite tamo u onoj kolibi — i pokaza rukom gde se nalazi sklonište popa Vlade Zečevića.

9 Odlomci iz pripovetke *Veče*

ANTONIJE ISAKOVIĆ

Znao sam da večera neće biti gotova još za dva sata te odlučih da to vreme provedem sedeći na kamenoj ploči.

Bio sam umoran, osećao sam u sebi neki pritisak kao izgladneo čovek. Nisam bio gladan, jer čim sam došao ponudili su me američkim sirom. Sekao sam nožem taj žuti sir u konzervi i mislio kako je za mene rat postao lakši. I sada to opet pomislih, videći pred štabom kako neka drugarica istresa ćebad. Spavaću na ćebetu koje neću nositi!

Dohvatih kamičak i bacih ga pred sebe.

Ispred mene stajale su dve mlade devojke. Tek sam ih onda video. Obe su bile iste visine, samo je jedna bila punija i imala je napred prebačene crne kike. Druga plašljiva i tanja, njenu kosu nisam video, bila je skrivena ispod bele marame.

Sigurno su me posmatrale odavno. Ona punija reče:

— Druže, možemo li s tobom da pričamo?

Pitanje me iznenadi: nije rekla da razgovaramo, nego da pričamo. Šta imamo da pričamo? Nespretno sam u ruci okretao duvansku kutiju.

— Možemo — rekoh.

One lako priđoše i sedoše do mene, jedna s jedne strane, druga s druge. Učini mi se da obe duboko dišu kao da su trčale.

Sada opazih da ona tanja nije tako crna kao punija. Da ima lepe, tamne oči i dugu poviju obrva. A punija je nadošla od snage divlje, mlade planinke. Obe su bile u belim težanim košuljama, samo je ona tanja imala na sebi kratku crnu bluzu.

— Vi ste sestre?

— Jesmo, samo ne rođene. Od stričeva.

— Ovo su naše kuće. — Tanja devojka ih pokaza rukom.

Ćutao sam i čekao da me one nešto pitaju. Ispod kamene ploče zrikavac je strigao. Daleko dole kretala se crna raž. U toj poljani raži odskakale su velike bele gomile — nabacano kamenje.

— Ono su gomile kamenja? — upitah.

— Čistimo njive, naša je zemlja takva. Vidiš onu najveću gomilu? Ove godine ja sam taj deo očistila — reče punija devojka.

— Kao grobovi — rekoh.

— Da, grobovi. — Devojka duboko uzdahnu.

Plašio sam se da ih nisam potsetio na poginule. Ovo je bila slobodna teritorija i svi sposobni muškarci bili su u partizanima. Naglo upitah:

— Ti se zoveš Gora?

— Ne, ali jesam kao gora — ona mrdnu ramenima — zovi me tako.

— A ti?

Tanja devojka uplašeno me pogleda i ja se iznenadih njenim odgovorom.

— Izmisli i za mene.

Rekoh prvo što mi pade na pamet.

— Tankostruka.

— Mnogo je dugačka.

— E onda ću te zvati: Katoda. Da li ti se to dopada?

— Čudno zvuči. A šta je to?

— To je nešto vižljasto, lepo.

— A meni si dao seljačko: Gora!

— Pa . . . sada ne bih umeo ništa drugo da izmislim. Možemo da razgovaramo i bez imena — brzo rekoh.

Iznenada Gora me upita:

— A rat, kad će da se završi?

— Pobedićemo!

— To znam, ali kada će da se završi? — gotovo uvređeno ponovi pitanje.

— Ne znam — i podigoh ramena.

— Ne znaš, pa ko onda treba da zna?

— Pa . . .

— Ove jeseni. — Devojka me uhvati za ruku.

— Pa sada je jesen!

— Ali tek je počela — i tanja me devojka uhvati za ruku.

— Da, počela, — prihvati Gora.

— Ali jesen je kod vas kratka.

— Pa dobro, hoće li se završiti ove zime?

— Ne znam.

— Reci: ove zime. Kakav si? Zima je kod nas duga. Čitavu šumu izgorimo, kako neće? — Obe devojke sa strahom su me gledale.

— Ako ne ove zime, onda iduće godine u ovo vreme gotovo je sa ratom.

— To je mnogo dugo — reče Gora i uhvati se za slabinu.

— Nije, proći će to brzo. A koga vi imate u ratu?

Ja se opet iznenadih odgovoru.

— Nikoga! — odgovoriše obe u glas.

— Kako?

— Nemamo braće. A momci kada su otišli, mi još nismo bile devojke — reče Gora.

— Sad ste devojke.

— Odavno.

Neko vreme smo ćutali i moje ruke bile su u njihovim. Ispod nas zrikavac je strigao.

— A ti odakle si? — Prvo pitanje koje mi uputi tanja devojka.

— To nije važno, vidiš da je naš.

— Hoću da znam. — I mene obradova ta njena upornost.

— Iz Srbije — odgovorih.

— Srbijanac — otegnuto reče devojka. — Mislila sam da su oni visoki.

— Ima nas raznih.

— A ti pre rata nisi dolazio u naše krajeve?

— Nisam.

— Naši ljudi su kod vas dolazili.

— Pa Srbija je bogata zemlja — reče ozbiljno Gora. — Šta kod nas ima? »Šipad«. I za naše nije bilo uvek mesta.

— A pre, znao si za naše krajeve?

— Učio sam u školi.

— Za Glamočko Polje?

— Da, za Glamočko Polje.

— Lepo je učiti školu — iskreno reče tanja devojka. — I sve si zamišljao da je kod nas ovako?

— Nisam.

— A šta nisi?

— Planine, mnogo su visoke.

— Naša učiteljica imala je veliku kartu i na njoj sam videla Srbiju.

— A ove vaše ratne mnogo su sitne — reče Gora. — Sve u njima ima, čak i naše kuće. Samo nema ove gde je smešten štab. Nju smo podigli prošle godine.

— Podigli? Čudno!

— Bilo je isečenih balvana — reče Gora.

— Dovukli smo građu od »Šipada« — reče devojka u crnoj bluzi. A otac kaže: balvane mogu i da odvuku, a zgradu ne mogu.

Ja se nasmejah.

U štabu je gorela karbituša. Oko njenog velikog plamena obletao je leptir.

Posmatrao sam Gorinu ruku i video na njenom srednjem prstu prost prsten.

— Prsten? — rekoh.

Ona klimnu glavom.

— Dobila si ga?

— Ne, naši momci su u ratu.

— I ja ga imam — reče devojka u crnoj bluzi.

— Dale smo ih jedna drugoj — suvo reče Gora. — Kod vas prsten isto znači?

— Da, ljubav — brzo odgovorih.

— Mi to ne znamo. — I obe se zagledaše dole u crno ražano polje.

Osećao sam njihove vruće dlanove kako počinju da me stežu. Počeh i ja polako da krećem ruke. Njihovi prsti milovali su moju ruku. U košulji osetih znoj oko kičme. Odmah sam pomislio što jedna od njih ne ode. One su i dalje sedele i gledale dole u raž koja je svilasto šuštala.

— Nema meseca — odjednom rekoh.

— Bolje je ovako — reče Gora.

— Izlazi tek oko ponoći — reče devojka u bluzi.

— Da nećeš otići? — upita me Gora.

— Kuda?

— Tamo — i ona pokaza glavom premu štabu.

— Neću.

— Ideš li noćas u stražu?

— Ne idem.

. . . . .

Neko je pred štabom palio baterisku lampu. Čas je puštao zeleno, crveno, pa belo svetlosno oko. Osvetljavao je neki sanduk.

Popušim cigaretu i mislim kako da se oslobodim jedne od njih. Izgledalo mi je da podjednako hoću obe. Opustih ruke i osetih kako ih one istog trenutka dograbiše. Devojka u crnoj bluzi milovala je nežnije a Gora gladnije, ljuće.

— Pije mi se voda — rekoh.

Pritajih disanje da bih po ruci poznao koja ce otići. Obe su gledale u moje čizme, u kratkoj tišini jasno se čula sva tri srca. Ja sa strahom ponovih:

— Žedan sam!

Obe naglo ustadoše.

— Sada ćemo doneti! — Ne znam koja je rekla.

Kada ostadoh sâm, očajan pružih noge i zapalih novu cigaretu. Pružio sam se preko celog stepenika, nešto me je golicalo oko vrata i želeo sam da se okupam u hladnoj vodi.

Devojke su dolazile i ja skupih noge. Gora je nosila bokal a druga zemljani sud.

— Nemamo šećera.

— Svejedno, žedan sam.

Obe ponovo sedoše i devojka u crnoj bluzi spusti pored sebe zemljani sud.

Krišom sam ih posmatrao da otkrijem nisu li između sebe što razgovarale. Povukoh se malo unazad i gledam njihova ukočena lica.

Posmatrale su jedna drugu, mrzele su se sada i nisam smeo da ih otvoreno gledam. Gorine poluotvorene usne slabo su se micale. Osećao sam da govori svojoj sestri: »Beži, što sediš tu. Starija sam, zaboravljaš to! Ja sam ga prva videla i on je moj.« Gora je savijala malo glavu i u njenim očima kupile su se sjajne gromuljice.

Devojka u crnoj bluzi gledala je začuđeno. Ona kao da je govorila: »Zašto se ljutiš na mene? Vidiš, voleo je i sa mnom da razgovara. Sa mnom je ozbiljnije pričao i dao mi najlepše ime, koje sam ja zaboravila. Misliš da miluje samo tvoju ruku? Hoćeš da kažeš da si starija? Ovde nema starije.«

Grickao sam usnu i mislio: hajde neka jedna od vas dve ode. Leva ili desna, svejedno. Možda bih ja trebalo da kažem. Kojoj da kažem? Ili da ustanem i pođem?

. . . . .

Vrata njihove kuće se otvoriše i osvetli nas ognjište. Po neravnom dvorištu titrale su naše nezgrapne senke. Video sam u sredini svoju najvišu i dva točka sa strane. Pred štabom videla se tri vojnika. Neko je otegnuto vikao moje ime.

— Nekog zovu — reče Gora.

— Da, zovu — nesvesno ponovih.

— Tebe?!

— Mene.

— Na večeru.

— Valjda — rekoh umorno.

Opet se čuo otegnut glas i vojnik je objašnjavao da me je video gore ispod borova.

Uskoro do nas poče da dopire zvek kašika i miris kuvanog krompira. Želeo sam da što pre prestanu da jedu. Neko je glasno hvalio kuvara. Pod nama je zrikavac ponovo počeo da striže, kamena ploča bila je još topla. Gora me povuče za ruku, savi se prema meni i ja spazih mrke pesnice u košulji. Pravo gleda u mene, osećam, hoće nešto da mi kaže. U sebi potiskuje reči, njeno grlo se nemo miče. Podiže ruku i široki rukav pade nadole.

— Vidiš onu moju gomilu. Sutra uveče biću tamo.

Obe sestre naglo se podigoše i odoše u kuću.

Ostao sam sâm i gledao u crno ražano polje, u veliku belu Gorinu gomilu kamenja. I čuo sam muziku. Vojnik je održao neku svoju reč. Sviralo je jako, bio je to jedan vojnički marš.

Opružio sam noge i ležao na širokom stepeniku. Neko je vikao:

— Kamo vesti!

Vojnik se branio da je našao talasnu dužinu.

— Menjaj! — drao se isti glas.

Onda je naišao zvuk klavira i šetao se oko drvenih kuća.

— Menjaj! — drao se glas, a ja sam želeo da klavir što duže ostane.

Ležao sam, pozadi mene borovi se pokretali, zrikavac je ućutao, a kamen je bio još uvek topao.

Sigurno sam dugo spavao. Mesec je goreo u ražanom polju. Ustadoh i brzo pođoh prema najvećoj gomili kamenja. Kod gomile spazih Gorina leđa i smolastu debelu pletenicu prebačenu do kukova. Mesec je zvonio nad poljem, mi smo stajali jedno pored drugog kad iz visoke raži izroni devojka u crnoj bluzi.

Opet smo sve troje sedeli i gledali u sjajnu raž.

10 Iz monologa *Moj sin*

IVAN SLAMNIG

Ima mnogo načina, na koje bi moj sin mogao živjeti. Zbilja, kad mislim o tim načinima, vidim da imam mnogo toga misliti.

Moj sin bi mogao biti negdje u Južnoj Americi. Mogao bi biti u jednom od onih zgodnih glavnih gradova koji se zovu Lima, Bogotá, Caracas. Ili Rio de Janeiro. U tom slučaju, on je obučen u bijelo odijelo, bijelo meko odijelo, u njem izlazi navečer na terasu — kad zamišljam Rio de Janeiro, uvijek je večer, a ljudi izlaze na prostrane terase u bijelim odijelima, vjetar puše s oceana ili La Plata ili već tako nečega, a ljudi u bijelim laganim smokinzima piju ledena pića. Komadi leda plivaju u zelenom kao krupni dragulji.

On nesumnjivo ima novaca. On ga zarađuje svojom sposobnošću. On ima tvornicu govedih konzervi, i on je jako bogat. I sad na terasi među svim tim lijepim ženama, od kojih bi svaka htjela njega, on obavlja poslove, poslovne razgovore. Smije se svojim južnjačkim okrutnim smijehom. On izgleda kao pravi Južnoamerikanac. Pri tome je tvrd, poslovan. Nije šala, steći za tako kratko vrijeme tako veliku tvornicu. Pogledaj ove zmijske oči blistavih žena oko njega. Čuvaj se, sine!

Možda ima neku odabranicu. Vjerujem da je znao dobro izabrati, premda bih voljela da sam i ja u tome učestvovala. Zapravo, ne znam da li bih voljela. Neka je izabere sâm. On ju je izabrao sâm. To je strankinja, ne razumijem, što ona govori, i mi ćemo se malo tuđiti jedna od druge, ali ja znam, da je to samo privremeno, a možda i prividno, jer koga moj sin voli, moram ga i ja voljeti. Da, on nalazi meni snahu, lijepu, bogatu.

Ima i drugih glasova, ima i drugih mogućnosti. To je priličan posao, zamišljati sve to skupa, ali je interesantno. Zapravo nije me briga ni da li je posao, ni da li je interesantno. Ja sjedim i

mislim o tome. Moram misliti, jer moram naći rješenje koje
sve zadovoljava. Ako analiziramo situaciju u Južnoj Americi,
mislim njegovu situaciju u Južnoj Americi, vidimo da ima
mnogo toga što nije baš u redu i našli bismo u toj mogućnosti
priličan broj pukotina. Moram još pažljivije razmotriti taj
slučaj.

Mogao bi biti i na nekom drugom mjestu. Mogao bi biti,
recimo, negdje na sjeveru, recimo u Norveškoj. Kad mislim o
tome bolje, čini mi se da je negdje daleko na sjeveru, hoda u
visokim čizmama i kožnoj mornarskoj olujnoj kapi. Po čemu
hoda? Mislim da hoda po gomili riba. On je vlasnik ribarskog
broda, on učestvuje u velikim lovovima na haringe i na bakalare
i na slične ribe, kojima tako obiluju ona sjeverna mora. Ne
znam što da mislim o tome, da je otišao u lov na kitove. Da,
moglo bi to biti. On je na kitolovcu otišao daleko negdje među
ledena brda. On viče i njegov glas odjekuje od jednog ledenog
brijega do drugog. On je već dugo, dugo na moru, on očekuje
neki specijalni ulov, on ima već neke svoje razloge. On i nije u
Norveškoj, on je negdje oko Južnog Pola. Tamo se sad naročito
love kitovi, rekli su mi. On je daleko negdje među ledom, on
vrši nekakav pothvat, znam da se radi o nečemu velikom, o
nekoj velikoj zaradi i slavi. Imao je, naravno, i neprilike, bio je
izgubljen u ledenoj pustoši, zimovao je jedamput ili dvaput
među ledenim santama, takve stvari se događaju, svi smo mi
već čuli za to. Ova mogućnost ima tu prednost, što se može naći
rješenje i tome, što se ne javlja.

Jer to je dosta važno pitanje. To treba imati u vidu.

(Možda njegov humak negdje u Bosni kiša oblijeva.)

On može biti i razmjerno sasvim blizu. Možda je u Italiji.
Možda čak u Trstu. Ne znam, kako je došao do novca. Mislim
— to „mislim" kažem radi vas, jer sam zapravo uvjerena, da
se u početku bavio malo švercom. Švercovao je cigaretama.
Ne može se uzeti da je neko zlo švercovati cigaretama. To je

luksuz, i tko ga je spreman skupo platiti, neka ga plati. Ako se već šverca, neka se šverca cigaretama. Ja bih ga razumjela i oprostila da je švercovao i čime drugim, ali najdraže mi je ipak što je švercao cigaretama. On je snalažljiv, hvala bogu, mislim da je to naslijedio po mojoj strani. Jedan moj brat je u tome vrlo sličan njemu. Morao je naći načina da dođe do novca, do dosta novca da može prijeći na veće pothvate, koji bi bili unosniji i časniji. Nisam se još odlučila da li u Trstu ima veliku trgovinu tekstila ili veliku trgovinu prehrambenih proizvoda. Bilo kako bilo, to je velika lijepa prostorija osvijetljena fluorescentnim cijevima, sve djeluje tako svježe, voćne konzerve i salame šarene se i svjetlucaju u vitrinama. U njegove trgovine dolazi samo bolji svijet. On sâm nije tako često unutra. Zna se, zapravo, kad šef dolazi u prodavaonicu. To znaju i stare mušterije, koje vole da ih baš on podvori. On je tu, stručnjak, brz i uslužan, a opet dostojanstven. Ima jedna ženska koja uvijek dolazi onda, kad je on u dućanu. Naručuje razne sitnice, uvijek neke gluposti. To ona dolazi radi njega, jasno. Oni izmjenjuju poglede dok on zamotava petnaest deka šunke. Ruke im se dodiruju. Ona bi htjela da ga ima. Mislim da se i ona njemu sviđa. Što se mene tiče, htjela bih znati nešto pobliže o toj djevojci. Danas se čovjek ne može ni u koga pouzdavati, a Trst je velik grad, u njemu ima svašta. Ne znam da li ona ljubi njegove bijele zube i crnu kosu, ili njegov dućan s tolikim naslagama skupih štofova.

Zadnji koji ga je vidio bio je neki Nedžad. Zadnji, koliko ja znam, naime. Od Nedžada potječe zadnja pouzdana vijest koju o njemu znam. Ovako Nedžad priča:

»Nas smo obojica bili u domobranima, a mislili smo preći u partizane. Bili smo u domobranima, a imali smo vezu s partizanima. Prelazili smo od jedne strane na drugu. Nas dvojica bili smo neka međuvojska.

Dugo vremena nije bilo nikakve veće gužve na onom terenu. Onda je najedamput onaj teren postao važan, došli su tamo

Nijemci, Čerkezi, četnici, ustaše, i svaki vrag, ne znam što im je bilo. I tako smo mi išli jednim putom. Tako smo došli do jedne velike lipe, gdje se put razdvajao. I onda je on rekao, »Ja ću ići lijevo, a ti hajde desno. Kad prođemo ovaj guštik, opet ćemo se sastati«. I tako je on otišao lijevo, a ja desno. I onda se ja nisam usudio izaći iz guštika, već sam tu ostao čitavo popodne i noćio sam, a sutra ujutru nije bilo ni od koga ni traga, pa ni od njega, i ja sam se do konca rata krio u svome selu, na sjeniku.«

Toliko je rekao Nedžad. Nitko nije posvjedočio ništa drugo. Koliko je Nedžad kod mene ispio crnih kava! A ipak nisam doznala kamo su išli, niti čega se on plašio u guštiku.

Jasno je da je on otišao n e k a m o. Nije ostao tamo. Najprije dolazi pitanje, kuda i kako je on otišao nekamo.

Najvjerojatnije je da je prebjegao u partizane. Interesirala sam se, koja je partizanska jedinica bila u to doba na tom terenu. Razgovarala sam s ljudima koji su mogli biti iz te jedinice. Oni su potvrdili da je na tom terenu bilo prebjegavanja. Interesirala sam se, naravno, upravo za svoga sina, opisivala sam ga, a oni su mi rekli da je moglo biti da je prešao netko tko bi odgovarao tome opisu. Prebjeglo ih je puno.

Doznala sam dalje da su neki ranjenici iz te jedinice bili prebacivani u Bari. Lako je moguće da su i njega prebacili u Bari. Lako je bilo moguće da je i on bio ranjen.

(Možda njegov humak negdje u Bosni kiša oblijeva.)

Iz romana *Daj nam danas*

RADOMIR KONSTANTINOVIĆ

Htela bih da igram, rekla je. Celog života sanjala sam da igram. Htela sam da odem na more, i da na nekoj hotelskoj terasi igram, više mora. Na svadbi isto nisam igrala. A sada bih ustala iz kreveta i otišla da igram. Sedeli smo za velikim stolom. Hoćeš da igramo? pitala sam ga. Ne, rekao je. Govorio mi je da ne voli da igra i da je umoran. Bio je bled i stalno me je gledao. Držao me je za ruku. Stiskao me je rukom ispod stola. Gazio me je. Imala sam bele cipele. I sva sam bila u belom, rekla je. Bojala sam se da ne isprlja moje cipele. Oko nas je bilo mnogo ljudi. Svi su došli. Smejali su se i vikali. On je bio zadovoljan. Hoću da se zna, govorio je, kako je kada se ženi Eduard Kraus. Onda se nagnuo nad mene. Da li ti je žao? pitao me je, što se nismo vozili fijakerom? Ja sam rekla da mi nije žao. (Ove violine, ove violine.) Kazala sam da hoću da igram. On je rekao da je hteo da idemo peške zato što je želeo da svi vide kakvu ženu je dobio Eduard Kraus. Neka vide, mrmljao mi je na uho. Ja hoću da igram, kazala sam. Gazio me je nogom. Boli me, kazala sam, i hoću da igram. On je rekao da je umoran. I ne možeš, rekao je, da igraš sa drugim. Danas si ti sa mnom. Danas je to drugo. Sasvim drugo. Sasvim drugo nego inače, rekao mi je. Znojio se. Zašto se toliko znojiš? pitala sam ga. On je odmahivao glavom. Ne znam, rekao mi je. Ovo se jednom dešava u životu — samo jednom, tvrdio je. Ja sam se nasmejala. A? rekla sam, zar si siguran? On je oborio glavu. Ubio bih te, rekao je, kada bi još jednom doživela ovo, sa nekim drugim. Ja sam se smejala. Bila sam ljuta što on neće da igra sa mnom. Drugi su igrali. Ja sam htela da igram kao drugi. Nisam htela da sedimo za stolom, da se držimo za ruke i da gledamo kako drugi igraju. Smejala sam se. Ne, rekla sam, mislila sam na to, da se ponovo venčamo.

Tako je lepo sada, kazala sam mu. Tako je lepo, rekla sam. Ustaću, odjednom sam mu kazala, i sama ću da igram ako ti nećeš. Smejala sam se. Oko nas su igrali. On je bio bled. Ne, ne, molio je, to ne smeš da učiniš, molio me je. Ja sam se smejala. Sama, sama, govorila sam. Videćeš. Onda me je on pogledao mutnim očima. Mislila sam da je pijan. Ja ne znam da igram, rekao je. Celoga života, rekao je, ja sam čekao ovaj dan. I ja nisam igrao, kazao je. Ja sam mislio da je lepo što nisam igrao, celoga života. Zar misliš da to nije lepo? Zar misliš da svaki čovek može da se pohvali time? upitao me je. Ne, rekla sam, i prestala da se smejem. Ne može svaki čovek da se pohvali time. Oko nas su još uvek igrali. Svirali su u trube, i na violine, i udarali u bubnjeve. Ja sam slušala i gledala sam, ali odjednom, to nije bilo kao ranije. Eduard i ja sedeli smo za onim velikim stolom. Na stolu bili su ostavljeni tanjiri, čaše za vino, činije, poslužavnici. Neko cveće. Mrve od hleba, ostaci od jela. Ugašene cigarete. Jedna cigareta dimila se. Ugasi je, rekla sam Eduardu. On kao da me nije čuo. Zurio je ispred sebe. Znala sam da ne može da vidi one koji igraju. Samo su igrali. Jedan čovek ležao je na dnu stola. Spavao je. Vino je bilo proliveno oko njegove glave. Odjednom mi se učinilo da su nas svi ostavili, da su nam svi kao neprijatelji i da smo Eduard i ja zauvek osuđeni na samoću. Između nas i ostalih bilo je veliko ćutanje, neka ravnodušnost. Možda neki hladni vazduh. Baš tako. Onda je, tamo, sa one strane tog ćutanja, tog hladnog vazduha, te ravnodušnosti, svirala muzika. Mi smo bili sami. Oni su igrali. Mo smo bili uplašeni, i držali smo se za ruke. Sami. Ugasi onu cigaretu, kazala sam ponovo Eduardu, i odjednom sam počela da plačem. Ljudi će da odu, mislila sam. I nisam znala da li je bolje da odmah odu i da se više nikada ne vraćaju tu, u te sobe, i da igraju, i da muzika svira, ili je bolje da ostanu još malo. Možda sam se bojala i od jednoga i od drugoga? Možda sam se bojala da ostanem nasamo sa Eduardom pored onog stola sa ostacima od hrane. Sve me je podsećalo na njih, na te ljude, na njih koji su bili zajedno. Plakala sam. Eduard me je uhvatio za ruke još čvršće. Ja ću da naučim da igram, govorio je, nemoj da plačeš. Ja ću da kupim gramofon, rekao je, videćeš. I onda ćeš da me naučiš da igram. To će da bude smešno, rekao je, biće vrlo, vrlo smešno i ti ćeš da se smeješ. Ja ću da igram i smejaćeš se. Ja ovako dugačak, šaptao je na moje uho, — i ovako smešan. Ali ja nisam nikada igrao, ja sam hteo da živim za ovaj dan. A ti plačeš, prošaptao je, kao da ja ne mogu da kupim gramofon, i kao da ti nećeš da me naučiš da igram. Ana, zovnuo me je kao da sam daleko od njega (a sedela sam uz njega i bili smo sami za onim velikim stolom). Ana, obećaj mi da ćeš da me naučiš da igram. Obećaj mi. Ja strašno volim da igram, kazao je. Obećaj mi.

Zaćutala je odjednom. Gledala je u mene, ali ja sam znao da me ne vidi. Videla je svadbu, sebe i Eduarda kako sede za jednim velikim stolom. Videla je kako drugi igraju. Eduard se zaklinjao da će da kupi gramofon. Šaputao je na njeno uho kako će da bude srećan kada bude igrao. (O, mnogo će onda da se smeje.) On je tako mislio. Ali nije sve bilo u tome. Ne, setio sam se, nije sve bilo u tome. Ona je osetila kako su sami. Odjednom kako su ostali sami, zauvek. — Hoćeš li da vidiš? upitala me je. Klimnuo sam glavom. Otišla je do ormana. Otvorila ga je i preturala nešto po njemu. Onda se vratila sa velikim paketom fotografija. Odrešila je plavu pantljiku koja je vezivala paket. Fotografije su se rasturile po stolu. Prebirala je po njima, tražila. A onda je našla fotografiju sa venčanja. Stepenici Saborne crkve. Sunce. Stajali su na tim stepenicima. Ana i Eduard u sredini. Ona je bila u beloj i dugačkoj haljini, sa cvećem u rukama. Smejala se. Izgledala je srećna. Ali ne, rekao sam u sebi; ona nije bila srećna. Da je bila, rekao sam, ne bi sada morala da se muči. Ležala bi mirno na krevetu. Gramofonska ploča se okretala. Violine i bubnjevi. Klavir. Njene oči su bile mutne. Nevidljivi fotograf mahao je svojim dugačkim, mršavim rukama. Bio je pognut, preko njegove glave padala je velika, crna krpa. Zurio je u staklo svog starinskog, drvenog fotografskog aparata na nogarima. On, nepriznati umetnik. On, koji je morao da oseti tajnu vremena, koji je pokušavao da zaustavi ljude u vremenu, u sreći i nesreći, koji se borio protiv tog vremena. Stari fotografe, šapnuo sam, ti koji si se borio protiv vremena. Šta je sa onim vremenom i gde se gube njegovi tragovi? Jednom čovek mora da bude srećan. Jednom mora da umre. Ali, zadrhtao sam, o kakvoj smrti govorim? Nema te smrti. Još jednom je tamo gde je Eduard Kraus. Ona je tamo gde je Ana. I doći će k njoj, rekao sam. Doći ce jednom. Pogledaj. Ona je držala cveće u rukama. Više nje stajao je jedan čovek. Smejao se. Drugi su se držali za ruke. Ana je čekala, napregnute pažnje. Cveće je svakog trenutka moglo da ispadne iz njenih ruku. Da se prospe.

Ali nisam ga naučila da igra, rekla je. I nikada nismo igrali. Posle je sve bilo kasno, prošaptala je. Bacila je fotografiju. Ja sam to znala. Znala sam da je kasno. Mogli smo da igramo. Mogli smo i da ne igramo, rekla je. Bilo je kasno. Jednog dana on je došao iz varoši i nosio je nešto. Ana, rekao je, doneo sam gramofon. A bilo je kasno. Ja sam to znala. Gramofon? pitala sam ga. Što si doneo gramofon? — Gledao me je ushićeno. Jadni Eduard. Zar si zaboravila? pitao me je. Hteo je da igramo. Možda je i on čuo neko more. Možda je i on razumeo da sa tom srećom treba da se svrši. Ali ne verujem. Ne, rekla sam ja njemu, sada ne možemo da igramo. Otišla sam u hodnik. Plakala sam. Jednom rukom sam se držala za zid, i plakala sam. Iza mene su se otvorila vrata. On je bio na njima. Okrenula sam se. Gledala sam ga. Bio je dugačak u svetlosti vrata. Napolju je varoš trubila. Varoš je pričala. Bio je strašno dugačak. Zar nećeš da igramo? prošaptao je. Vrati se da igramo, kazao mi je. Ne, rekla sam, ne, ne, Eduarde, kazala sam mu, kako to ne možeš da razumeš? Ne, kazala sam mu.

Uzdahnula je. — Odbila sam ga, kazala je.

12 Iz pripovijetke *Čudo u Olovu*

IVO ANDRIĆ

Svitalo je kad su izišli na prve visove iznad Sarajeva. Djevojčica, koja se dotle mnogo žalila, nećkala i plakala, sad je počivala u jednom naročito udešenom plitkom sepetu, koji su nosili momci na dvije sohe provučene sa strane. Zamorena i opijena svježinom, spavala je, sa glavom na desnom ramenu. Pokatkad bi, kod potresa, otvarala oči, ali videći nad sobom zeleno granje, nebo i rumen sjaj, ponovo bi ih zatvarala, i misleći da sanja, smiješila se finim smiješkom bolesna djeteta koje se oporavlja.

U neko doba prestade uspon. Prolazili su gustim šumama, a put je bio širi i blaži. Tu već počeše da susreću, u skupovima, svijet iz ostalih mjesta. Bilo ih je teško bolesnih, koji su, natovareni kao vreće na konje, muklo ječali i kolutali očima. Bilo je i ludih i bjesomučnih, koje su rođaci pridržavali i smirivali.

Stara Bademlićka je išla ispred svojih, probijala se između svijeta, i, ne gledajući ni u koga, molila šapatom krunicu. Nosači su je jedva stizali. Dvaput su se odmarali u bukovoj šumi pored puta. Za vrijeme ručka prostriješe po travi zagasit iram i na njega položiše bolesnicu. Ona je protezala utrnule noge i zgrčen stas, koliko je mogla. Prepade se kad pored sebe vidje majčine noge, bose, pomodrele, i sve krvave od nenavikla puta. Ali stara uvuče brzo noge pod dimije, a djevojčica, radosno zbunjena tolikim novim stvarima oko sebe, zaboravi odmah na to. Sve je bilo novo, neobično i radosno: gusta i tamna šumska trava, teške bukve, sa pečurkama kao policama na srebrnastoj kori, ptice koje su padale konjima na zobnice, i širok vidik sa svijetlim nebom i duguljastim oblacima koji sporo brode. I kad bi konj odmahnuo glavom i ptice poletele ustrašene oko njega, djevojčica je, iako umorna i sanjiva, morala da se smije, dugo i tiho. Gledala je kako momci jedu sporo i ozbiljno, i u tom je takođe bilo nešto smiješno i veselo. I sama je slatko jela. Pružala se na svom ćilimu koliko je više mogla. Razgrnuvši rukom hladnu travu, ugleda cvijet, zvan babino uho, sitan i jarko crven, pri crnoj zemlji, kao izgubljen. Viknu lako od uzbuđenja. Stara, koja je bila od umora zadrijemala, prenu se i ubra joj ga. Mala ga je dugo gledala i mirisala, držeći ga na dlanu, a onda ga pritisnu na obraz, i kad osjeti kako je kadifast i hladan, zaklopi oči od slasti.

Predveče stigoše u Olovo. Oko manastirskih ruševina i presvođenog basena, iz koga se muklo čulo kako pada topla voda Gospina Vrela, bio je cio jedan vašar svijeta. Gorile su vatre, peklo se, kuvalo i jelo. Većina je spavala na ravni. U jednoj daščari je bilo mjesto za imućnije i bolje. Tu se smjestiše Bademlićevi. Obje žene su ubrzo čvrsto zaspale. A djevojčica je cijelu noć provela kao u nekom polusnu, gledala kroz prozor zvijezde nad crnom šumom: toliko zvijezda koliko ih nikad nije vidila. Osluškivala je glasove koji svu noć nisu prestajali da žamore oko vatara, i tako se zanosila u san; pa bi je onda konjsko rzanje ili noćna svježina budili; slušajući ponovo žagor i glasove, nije mogla nikako da se razabere i da sazna: kada sanja i kad je budna.

Sutra u rano jutro odoše vrelu.

Prvo se ulazilo u jednu nisku i polumračnu sobu, u kojoj se svlačilo. Podnice su bile mokre i natrule. Pored zidova su stojale drvene klupe na kojima su ostavljane haljine. Odatle se niz tri drvena basamaka silazilo u veću i malo svjetliju prostoriju u kojoj je bio basen. Sve je bilo od kamena. Krov je bio kamenit, sveden, a visoko pri vrhu bili su mali okrugli otvori, kroz koje je padala čudna svjetlost u mlazevima. Koraci su odjekivali i kameni svod je uvećavao i vraćao svaki i najmanji zvuk. Šum vode odbijao se od svodova, i umnogostručen i uvećan ispunjao cio prostor, tako da se moralo vikati pri govoru. A ta vika se opet lomila i udvajala pod svodovima. Isparavanje je otežavalo dah. Sa zidova i svodova je milila voda, ispod koje se hvatala zelena siga, kao u pećinama.

Voda je padala u debelom mlazu iz jednog kamenog oluka. Bila je topla, bistra, puna srebrnastih mjehurića; razlivala se po kamenom basenu, i tu je od sivih ploča dobivala zelenkastu boju.

Naizmjence su se kupali, muškarci pa žene. Kad je došao red na žene, nastade guranje, prepirka i dozivanje. Jedne su odjevene, samo se izule i gaze vodu, koja im je do iznad koljena, druge se skinule sve do košulje. Nerotkinje čuče, do vrata u vodi, i zaklopljenih očiju se mole. Neke hvataju vodu s mlaza u dlanove i ispiraju grlo, uši i nozdrve. I svaka je toliko zauzeta molitvom i mišlju o ozdravljenju, da niko ni od koga ne zazire, kao da jedna drugu i ne vide. Malo se pogurkaju, i porječkaju se radi mjesta, pa odmah opet zaborave i svoju prepirku i jedna drugu.

Stara Bademlićka i zaova joj uvode djevojku u vodu. Iako su svi zaneseni i zabavljeni svak o sebi, opet svi prave mjesta, jer bogat i otmen svijet ne gubi nikad i nigdje svoje prvenstvo.

Onako zgrčena, djevojka drhti i boji se vode i svijeta. Ali se pomalo sve dublje spušta u vodu, kao da želi da se sakrije. I, da je ne pridržavaju ispod pazuha, ona bi sjela na dno. I ovako joj je voda dolazila do podbratka. Nikada u životu nije vidila toliko vode ni čula toliko glasova, i čudne jeke. Samo pokatkad, kad bi usnila da je zdrava, da može da hoda i trči, sanjala je da se sa ostalom djecom kupa u nekoj vodi, i da joj po tijelu poigravaju, ovako kao sada, bezbrojni, svijetli i sitni mjehurići. Zanosila se. Sklapala je oči i brzo udisala toplu paru iz vode. Kao iz sve veće daljine čula je glasove žena oko sebe. Osjeti kako je nešto golica po očima. Steže čvršće vjeđe, ali golicanje ne prestade. Konačno s mukom otvori oči. Kroz jednu od onih okruglih rupa na svodu prodirao je mlaz sunca i padao njoj na lice. U svjetlu je titrala i dizala se vodena para, kao sitna prašina, zelena, modra i zlatna. Bolesnica je išla pogledom za njom. Odjednom zadrhta i trznu se nekoliko puta, pa poče sa naporom da se diže iz vode. Iznenađene, majka i tetka joj počeše da je puštaju, pridržavajući je sve slabije. A zgrčena i uzeta djevojčica odjednom se ispravi, kao nikad dotle, pusti ruke koje su je podržavale sa strane, i, još uvijek malko pognuta, pođe polagano i nesigurno kao malo dijete. Raširi ruke. Na tankoj i mokroj košulji se ukazaše malene dojke tamnorumenih vrhova. Između teških trepavica bljesnu vlažan sjaj. Pune usne se razvukoše u neočekivan tup i čulan osmijeh. Podiže glavu, i, zagledana gore, visoko, u onaj mlaz svjetla, viknu odjednom nekim neočekivano jasnim i prodirnim glasom:

— Eno ga, silazi na oblacima! Isuse, Isuse! Aaah!

13 Iz knjige *Na putu*

PETAR ŠEGEDIN

Mladić je već bio pojeo svoj objed; zaposlio se promatranjem mene. Moju smirenost prekinuo je novi gost: srednji gospodin, čvrsta, zbita tijela i isto tako zatvoreno oblikovana, crnpurasta lica s oštrim četkastim brkom tek nešto prosjedim. Kretao se energično u dobrom — malo ponošenom — odijelu, a našao se neočekivano uz naš stol i kao usput tek, tek toliko da bi izvršio formalnost, pitao je dozvolu da sjedne. Prije nego što mu je moj susjed išta rekao, on je već sjeo i počeo glasno zvati konobara. Nismo ga zanimali, osjećalo se ipak da zna kako ga gledamo, no on kao da je bio nad tim. Konobar se nije mogao odmah javiti, i on se vidljivo uzrujavao. Konačno se približio i konobar, kazao mu koja su još jela preostala, ali on ga nije htio slušati, već je uporno tražio »kartu«, nek mu se donese »karta«, on jede »à la carte«. Konobar mu je donio »kartu«, gost se počeo prepirati s njim i kada mu je već po treći put bilo rečeno da je zakasnio, on je superiorno odmahnuo rukom zureći i dalje u papir, vjerojatno čitajući i učeći napamet sve ono, što se danas moglo dobiti u hotelu. Konačno je dobio isto jelo koje je bilo i meni servirano.

Mladi se moj susjed smirio; kao da mu je novi gost pomogao u snalaženju: pogledao me i sada već vidljivo htio uspostaviti dodir. Naši su osjećaji bili isti prema novom gostu. Držao sam se pasivno, i mladić je počeo osjećati da je sâm: zbunjenost se ponovo ocrtavala, iskre diskretnog prijekora javljale su se u njegovim plavim očima. Još jedno tamno iskustvo više u njegovu životu: i on se počeo zatvarati. Spoznao sam jasno taj svoj propust. Ništavan možda u razvoju tog lica, a možda je jedan od onih trenutaka, koji odlučuju . . . Da bih se spasio od neugodna čuvstva, svrnuo sam pažnju na novog gosta. Njegovo mesnato lice, zaposleno oko hranjenja, nametalo mi je neposredno poređenje s licem mladićevim.

Novi je gost bio posve zaokupljen svojim jelom. S vidljivom ugodnošću on je pregledao tanjur, viljuške, žlicu, nož, čaše, i valjda mu se nož nije svidio, otklonio ga je na stranu i izvadio svoj džepni nožić, otvorio ga, očistio oštricu palcem i kažiprstom, te počeo njim rezati svoj komad mesa. Ni jednim znakom nije odavao da se brinuo za svoju okolinu: zatvoren i okružen svojim interesom, u kretnjama, u svojoj ljubavi za sve svoje, on je u meni budio strah, koji su budili svi ljudi, za koje sam ustanovio da je nemoguć dodir, negdje na ljudskoj liniji. Sistematičnost, savršenost u kretnji, u nebrizi za čitavu okolinu, davali su i izraz tom licu: gotov čovjek, ali kakav čovjek . . .

Svrnuo sam pogled k drugom susjedu, no on je gledao prema prozoru. Htio je otići: zvalo ga je sunce i slobodan prostor — ali neka, vjerojatno lijena, ustrajnost zadržavala ga je na stolici.

S jedne strane gotov čovjek, a s druge nov putnik u život . . .

14　Iz romana *Zlo proljeće*

MIHAILO LALIĆ

Često smo se nalazili u ljubičastim jarugama ispod učiteljeve kuće. Pod zaštitom makijastog sitnog žbunja ostalo je tu još nešto trave, a koze su se zanimale glogovim omladima. I ja sam se tu dobro osjećao — tako u blizini, pritajenoj i skoro bolnoj od čežnje i nevjerovatnih sanjarija — u istom vazduhu koji Vidra diše, da gledam drveće i rječne okuke koje ona gleda.

Taj kraj izgledaše mi izuzetan na svijetu i ne znam kako sam se divio učitelju Jasikiću što je voćke posadio i postavio plotove. Sve to nije se moglo zamisliti jedno bez drugog i kao da mu se nije imalo šta dodati ni oduzeti: crveni krov i stakla što blješte iznad vijenaca zelenila punog košnica i jabuka i gdje bijelim debelim slapom šiklja voda iz dubokih zemljanih žila.

A Branku se od svega toga samo jabuke sviđahu. On ih je praćkom obarao i one bi se dokotrljale do plota, ranjene i sočne, mirišljive. Hvalio se njihovom ljepotom kao da ju je on sâm stvorio i nikad nije pomislio da je to nedozvoljen način i da se treba uzdržati, jer on ih nije obarao da ih jede nego da ih daje drugima. On je volio samo da nešto radi, da postiže, da zaposli ruke.

Bile su to nemirne i samovoljne ruke, koje kao da su imale neki svoj poseban mozak i nikad nijesu ostavile vremena mišljenju da ih stigne i spriječi u onome što im se prohtjelo. Njegove ,,puškare" i štrcaljke od zove zadale su mnogo glavobolje učitelju Jasikiću, i onda je napravio jednu malu vodenicu na potoku i pričaše se da njegove ruke stvore sve što mu oči vide, ali on je pravio i više od toga: neke viseće jazove iz kojih kroz probušeni žlijeb kapljice u pravilnim razmacima, kao sat, zvone padajući na podmetnut limeni listić.

Nadao sam se da će tu izrasti darovit inžinjer, ali ne bi ništa od toga. On ne izdrža ni mjesec dana u gimnaziji: zavadi se s varoškom djecom oko lopte, satjera ih u ćošak kod džamije i, jurišajući na njihov zaklon, polomi prozore nekom trgovcu; bio je u tu kavgu uvukao i Nenada Lukinog i još neke — sve ih istjeraše po 42 paragrafu kao da su jedva dočekali tu gužvu. On se ne ozlojedi na to i kao da odahnu: ,,Sad sam slobodan građanin", reče, pa time utješi i druge koji su iz raznih razloga morali da napuste školu.

A ja sam i dalje ostao bez slobode, i to dvostruko. I ta jesen, kad propadaše mnogo stoke na trgovima gdje niko nije htio da je kupi — meni je izgledala lijepa. Svakog dana viđao sam Vidru — uveče, kad se vraćamo iz škole. Strah od mraka zbijao nas je u gomilu koja prelazi svoje kilometre i pjesmom skraćuje put. Jedne noći zadrža nas neki posao u varoši, mislim da je to bio baš njen posao — nekakvo kupovanje — i mi zakasnismo: ona i Jug Jeremić i ja.

Mjesec uskoro zađe. Vedra i prohladna noć sa šuštanjem opalog lišća. Lim, plitak, bješe se slegao pod obalom i utišao se pun zvijezda. Svijetljahu ognjišta u prekolimskim selima kao da su i to zvijezde, a psi, siti — jer se svud klalo — javljahu se spokojno da prekrate tišinu. Onda Jug svrati kod ujaka da tamo prenoći, jer bliže mu je tako, a nas ostavi same. Ja mislim da je on to namjerno učinio, ali mi o tome nijesmo nikad govorili.

Tada — kao da me izdade glas. Ukočen u ustima i odrvenio, jezik mrtav ležaše. I ja otada ništa ne rekoh, a ni ona. Išli smo i išli kroz tu zvijezdanu noć — kamenje s drvećem govoraše oko nas različitim glasovima, a ja sam slušao kako mi srce tuče pomamno i bojao sam se da će ga ona čuti, a ništa nijesam mogao učiniti da ga utišam.

Najzad stigosmo do česme pred njihovom kućom. I ona reče:

,,Doviđenja!"

To je bilo tihim glasom, tako sličnim šumorenju da se i sad

čudim kako sam mogao zapamtiti to što se jedva razlikuje od onoga tihog šuma kojim se odvaja list od grane kad opada.

Sjećanje je čudna stvar i ja, koji sam pozaboravljao mnoge grmljavine, i sad kao da čujem onaj šumor opet i opet kako se ponavlja. Pa i ako neće biti novog viđenja, bar taj trenutak neću da pustim da mi ode nikad, nikad — dogod mogu da ga tako oživljavam.

15 Iz romana *Tišine*

MEŠA SELIMOVIĆ

Prolazi dan, dva, tri, ne znam koliko, a ja čekam da se nešto desi. Siguran sam da će se desiti, radost neka, ljubav, ma šta što nije mrzovoljno sivilo dana i noći. Čudno, kažem sebi, da se nisam suviše naglo zaustavio? Ratni kovitlac je odjednom stao i sad ne mogu da podesim korak.

Nepovratno se osjećam kao beskućnik. Nije to sasvim loše, nemam obaveza ni ograničenja, samo je pomalo prazno. Svejedno mi je kuda ću poći kad završim posao. Uvijek sam želio tu potpunu slobodu, a nikud ne polazim, nijednu mogućnost ne iskorišćujem, niti zapravo znam kakve su. Hodamo bez cilja, tražimo se, a kad se nađemo, govorimo o ratu.

Nijedno mjesto nije naše, ne znamo da ga osvojimo, kao da ćemo otići nekud. U kafani je krš uniformi, gunjeva, oštrog vonja, dima, glasnih razgovora, razmetljivo nevesela gužva u kojoj se osjeća da teren nije ni naš ni tuđi. Još ga preziremo, ne sklanjamo noge u čizmama i teškim cokulama, s visoka gledamo kelnere što se vuku bezvoljno, gotovo s gađenjem. I oni preziru nas, nesavijanjem leđa, podignutom obrvom, prljavom bluzom, rastresenošću. Još se ne snalazimo ni mi ni oni. Kelner je negdje daleko u mislima, odvojen od nas, zagledan u veliki prozor što se trese zbog tenka u prolazu.

— Kafu — zamolih ponovo.

— Molim, čuo sam.

Ironija u profesionalnoj učtivosti, prezir koji jedva krije. Oči su mu drevne: kroz njih su prošle hiljade ljudi i svaki je ocijenjen u djeliću sekunde. Mi novi, ocijenjeni smo zajedno, nije nas vrijedilo izdvajati ponaosob.

Kafa je loša, mlaka, neukusna.

— Nemate bolju kafu?

Kelner je sijao od sreće:
— Nemamo. Još jednu, molim?
— Ne.
— Pa? — pita Duško. — Šta si radio ova tri dana?
— Zar su već tri dana?
— Brzo ti je prošlo?
— Nije brzo prošlo.
Pričam o lasici, on se veselo smije. Pita:
— Je li ružna?
— Nije ružna.
— Pa zašto onda? Mlada, lijepa, što nisi ostao?
— Nije više ona nekadašnja.
— Baš zato. Sad si joj potrebniji.
— Ne volim samilost.
— A zamisli da ste se vjenčali prije rata?
— Šta bi bilo?
— Ne znam.
Čekam da kaže sve, ali on zaćuti. Ne znam šta krije, i neću
da pitam. Bolje ovako. Ne volim ni svoje ni tuđe ispovijedanje.
Onda mu pričam o redakciji. Urednik me dočekao tako
srdačno da sam već pomislio da je zabuna. Ali nije bila zabuna,
znao je ko sam, sretali smo se i poznavali za vrijeme rata, ali ne
za ovoliku srdačnost. Uostalom, tako sam ja mislio, on nije:
poznavao me tako temeljito da sam se zaprepastio. Doduše,
poznavao je svakoga. Dok smo sjedili u kancelariji, ušlo je
mnogo ljudi, kao u kafanu, niko se ne najavljuje. I svakog je
zvao po imenu, udarao ga po ramenu, pitao za poznanike, a
ljudi su se zbunjivali, iako nisam znao zašto.
Udarao me po mišicama, kliktao, vikao ah i oh, i — drago mi
je, i — gdje si tako dugo, onda telefonom poručio dva čaja, jača.
Pitao me:
— Da li još voliš jači čaj?
Nikad nisam volio ni da vidim čaj, ni jači ni slabiji, i kažem
izvinjavajući se:
— Više volim kafu.

— Kafu — poručio je razočarano. I malo začuđeno, čini mi si. Ali opet je uhvatio ravnotežu:

— Pa kako u tvom Užicu?

— Ja nisam iz Užica.

— Ah, da, iz Kragujevca.

Nisam bio ni iz Kragujevca.

— E tako — nastavio je već pomalo nervozno, iako se smješkao. — Drago mi je što ćemo raditi zajedno. Konačno ćeš moći da se baviš svojom strukom.

Sa strahom očekujem da čujem šta mi je struka. Nije me ostavio dugo u neizvjesnosti:

— Privreda, čini mi se?

To mi je struka koliko i Sanskrit. Ali ćutim. Ako se opet pobunim, ispašće da se uopšte ne poznajemo, ili da je on u potpunoj zabludi, ne znam šta je gore. I glupavo gledam u njega pokušavajući da zadržim normalan izraz lica, čak sam se i smješkao, iako s naporom, misleći kako nije uvijek lako s ljudima koji sve znaju. Ali sam, izgleda, pretjerao u nastojanju da ga uvjerim kako je sve u redu, i on je počeo da me gleda sumnjičavo.

— Ili nije?

Znao sam da se to sakato pitanje odnosi na moju struku, ali je zvučalo prijeteći. Mučio sam se: priznati ili ne priznati. Odgovorio sam sakato, prema njegovom kalupu:

— Jezik.

— Ruski? — upitao je s posljednjom nadom.

— Francuski.

— Završen fakultet?

— Ne.

— A, tako. Dobro, vidjećemo.

Duško se smijao mojoj priči.

— Sve si izmislio — kaže.

— Ne baš sve. Recimo pola.

On se opet smije, sad već s manje opravdanja i duže

nego što bi trebalo. A kad ućuti, gleda u pepeljaru, i kaže neodređeno:

— Da, da.

— Šta: da, da.

— Ništa. Čini mi se da si nezadovoljan. Možda si očekivao nešto drugo.

— Očekivao sam da budem guverner Narodne banke.

Nasmijali smo se, ali sam osjetio uznemirenost. I krivo mi je, kao da me zatekao na ružnom djelu. A stvarno nisam mislio o tome, nisam zamjerao svom neodređenom položaju koji može da bude samo skroman, nisam imao čak ni nekih planova ni želja, svejedno mi je, šta bih ja s položajem i šta bi on sa mnom, smiješno je i zamisliti. Ako sam očekivao povjerenje, to je prirodno, vjerovao sam u sebe, kao i svi koji se ni na čemu nisu okušali. Nama su sva vrata otvorena, sve želje ostvarive, sve mogućnosti nadomak, treba samo htjeti, a ja hoću. Svejedno je odakle ću početi, negdje će izbiti ova nagomilana osjećajnost s kojom se teško nosim, jer još ne znam čemu da je podredim. Nekome će biti potrebno ono što budem učinio, neko će zastati pred tim i pogledaće me začuđeno: zaista, to je tvoje djelo? Još ne znam kakvo je to djelo, ali ma kakvo da bude, biće lijepo.

Duško me gleda, smiješi se da izbriše moguću nelagodnost zbog svoga pitanja:

— O čemu misliš?

— Obezličio me nekako. Osjećao sam se kao da nemam korijena ni staništa.

— O kome govoriš?

— O uredniku.

— Vrlo važno.

— Dabome.

— Mislim to što urednik kaže. Hoćeš li da odemo nekud?

— Kuda?

— Kud bilo. Da pijemo, da bjesnimo.

— Zašto?

— Onako. Ako hoćeš.
— Neću. Ne osjećam nikakvu potrebu.
— Onda je sve u redu.
— Sve je u redu.

16 *Kasni posjetilac*

NIKOLA ŠOP

Ušao je baš u času kad su uzvanici u dvorani zašutjeli. Svi su čuli njegov ulazak. Prigušen škrip brave. I gušenje koraka u dubokom sagu.

Sad će ući. Već se čuje svlačenje kaputa i puckanje dugmadi. I povlačenje češlja u kosi. Da, sad se sigurno pogledao još jednom u ogledalu.

I evo, ulazi.

Ali, njega još nema. Šta radi? Svima je već sumnjiv. Da i tu ne pretražuje kapute? Bilješke traži. Nakite, tajna pisma. Ili ga opijaju odjeci mirisa zaostalog u dnu ženskih šešira.

Posjetilac se uplašeno obazre. Prisluškuje. Sad, ovog trenutka, mora svršiti onaj tajni posao. Jer inače će biti zatečen, uhvaćen. Užasno. Mogao bi se pojaviti uslužni domaćin ili neki udomaćeni gost da vide što radi, i da ga uvedu. Da ga uvedu onako nespremnog. Stajao bi usred društva sav obamro, usplahiren i potpuno nag.

Sad mora, mora ući. Tajni posao je svršen. Odluka je pala. Brzo s lica kao da nešto skida i baca u neku tajnu škrinju, a iz druge nešto opet izvadi i navuče na lice. Tako. Sad je miran. Još jednom priđe ogledalu. Više se ne prepoznaje.

Nitko od gostiju ne zna što je uradio kasni posjetilac. A svaki je to isto učinio, kad je odlagao svoj šešir i ogrtač. O tome se sada šuti, jer kad bi se otkrila tajna, bezobzirno bi jedan drugom zgulio s lica obrazinu koju je kradom navukao u predsoblju.

Zakašnjeli posjetilac napokon uđe smiješeći se.

17 *Gost strašilo*

NIKOLA ŠOP

Šta je bilo u licu toga čovjeka, da su ga se svi bojali, izbjegavali ga i potajno mrzili? Još izdaleka svaki ga je gost prepoznavao po koraku. I za tren, već je banuo u dvoranu ne odloživši u predsoblju ni kaput ni šešir, nego je sve ostavljao negdje u zakutku dvorane.

— Kakva drskost! Kakvo divljaštvo! — gnjevno zašapću uzvanici. I ništa više, jer bi mogao čuti.

Odmah zatim, svi se stanu natjecati da mu se što više približe. Da ga obaspu što laskavijim riječima. Da mu osmjehom, stiskom ruke i očima suznim od uzbuđenja izraze divljenje.

Pa onda: pritrčavanja, ponude, donošenje najboljih jestiva i pića, koja su samo za njega čuvana. I napokon, jednoglasno i urnebesno priznanje da je jedino on dostojan da sjedi u začelju stola.

Ali iz svih osmijeha, klanjanja i divljenja izbivao je skriven strah i odvratnost prema tome čovjeku.

Zašto ga tako mrze? Zašto im je njegovo lice tako sjajno da zaklanjaju oči? Zašto pred njim strepe od pritajenog užasa? . . .

Jer je među njih došao — bez obrazine.

Rastreseni gost

NIKOLA ŠOP

Usred najživljeg razgovora, u kome je vodio prvu riječ, naglo mu zape u grlu i potamni.

Nečije ga oči neumoljivo i zgranuto promatraju.

Osjeti nesvjesticu, kovitlanje i maglenje pred sobom sve tamnije i — sruši se u nesvijest. Još je samo čuo uzbunu, muklu jurnjavu, zvonki pad čaše i onda — mir.

Zatim, kao da roni iz dubine, sve bliže nekoj svijetloj površini, sve bliže vedrini, poče disati i srkati mlaz osvježenja. Plašljivo otvori oči.

Nad njim nagnuta mnoga lica. Ruke ga čvrsto pridržavaju. I začu se nečiji glas:

— Gospodine, šta vam se to dogodilo? Uzmite još vode. Bit ćete opet svježi.

On ustane, osmijehom se zahvali i zamoli da mu oproste, što je nesretnim slučajem uznemirio društvo.

Iako su svi navalili i usrdno ga molili da ostane, on se je ipak oprostio sa svima i otišao kući. Morao je tako učiniti, jer bi inače doživio potpuni slom.

Odmarajući se u naslonjaču za svojim stolom, nije se mogao samome sebi dovoljno načuditi:

Zar on da bude tako zaboravan, tako neoprezan! On, koji je uvijek bio zagonetan svima i uvijek privlačan baš zbog svoje tajnovitosti.

Ne, još se nikako ne može snaći. Uzalud utješne riječi što ih govori samome sebi. Uzalud sva zavaravanja, da nitko nije primijetio njegovu zlokobnu rastresenost. Možda i nije, jer zašto su ga, kad je izronio iz nesvijesti, zapitkivali:

— Gospodine, šta vam se to dogodilo?

Nitko dakle nema ni pojma. Nitko i ne sluti.

Ali samo jedan gost. Samo onaj koji je cijelo vrijeme bio nepomičan i šutljiv. Još uvijek mu je pred očima njegov oštri i pronicavi pogled. Taj pogled od kojeg se je onesvijestio. I taj užasni šapat, koji će ga vječno progoniti.

Šapat: — Bijedniče, prozreo sam te. Našao sam u predsoblju zaboravljenu — tvoju obrazinu.

19   Iz članka *Grad slavne prošlosti*

iz časopisa *Revija*

Istorija ukazuje da je već oko godine 1000 Zagreb morao biti prikladan gradić, jer je odlukom hrvatskog kralja Ladislava već u XI stoleću odabran za sedište kršćanske biskupije, jedne od prvih katoličkih biskupija na Balkanu. U jednom sredovečnom spisu uz godinu 1094 spominje se ime Zagreba — u latinskom obliku „Zagrabia", pa je tako Zagreb dobio svoj hiljadugodišnji krsni list.

Nekoliko stoleća kasnije odigrao je Zagreb, vojnički dobro utvrđen, za povest Evrope svoju najznačajniju ulogu. Upravo pod njime i na prostoru oko njega, zaustavljena je i slomljena stoletna otomanska invazija u Evropu. Turci su nekoliko puta opsedali Zagreb, ali njegova čvrsta utvrđenja — deo zidova vidljiv je i danas — nikada nisu uspeli savladati. Održava se i danas tradicija da se na spomen jednog uzmaka Turaka svakog dana u 14 sati oglašava posebno zvono sa stolne crkve.

20   Iz članka *Novembar u Beogradu*

iz časopisa *Revija*

Kada su 20. oktobra 1944. godine jedinice Narodno-oslobodi-
lačke vojske oslobodile Beograd u njemu je bilo manje od
300.000 stanovnika — manje nego što je u njemu živelo pre
rata. Danas, Beograd sa širim područjem ima preko miliona
stanovnika, što znači da svaki dvadeseti Jugosloven živi u ovom
gradu.

Odmah po oslobođenju Beograđani su se sukobili sa ogromnim teškoćama. U polusrušenom gradu nije bilo osnovnih
uslova potrebnih za život stotine hiljada ljudi. Izuzetnim
poletom, ne samo Beograđana, nego i cele zajednice, prebrođene
su prve teškoće. Grad je rastao i širio se, a danas je najveći i
najlepši od svog postanka. Sve značajnije stambene građevine
podignute su u Beogradu posle oslobođenja. Gotovo filmskom
brzinom nicale su nove četvrti. Ono što se pre samo nekoliko
godina smatralo za daleku gradsku periferiju danas su moderna
naselja. Dečji vrtići, škole, centri zdravstvene zaštite, bioskopi,
tržnice, podižu se uporedo sa novim stambenim četvrtima.

Na desnoj obali Dunava, preko Save, nikao je nov grad.
Na močvarnom i peskovitom tlu omladinske brigade iz cele
zemlje 1948. godine udarile su temelje Novom Beogradu.

Novi Beograd presecaju novi bulevari. Objekti na koje se u
početku malo mislilo niču u sve većem broju. Hoteli, moderne
tržnice, sportske hale, zdravstveni objekti projektovani po svim
pravilima savremene arhitekture danas su već stvarnost.

21 Iz članka *Titograd*

iz časopisa *Revija*

Tek od 1946. godine, kada je na ruševinama Podgorice počeo da niče Titograd, grad je počeo da poprima konture modernog naselja. Imao je sve uslove da postane glavni grad Crne Gore. Smešten ja na raskrsnici puteva koji vode prema moru i u unutrašnjost zemlje. Titogradski aerodrom povezan je vazdušnim linijama sa svim većim centrima u zemlji.

Ako sâm Titograd, kao novi grad, nema zanimljivih starih spomenika, njegova okolina u tom pogledu je veoma privlačna. Na dvanaestom kilometru od grada nalazi se jedno od najstarijih utvrđenja u zemlji — Medun, koje potiče iz IV veka pre naše ere. Podigli su ga Grci na jednom brežuljku. Međutim, najveća atrakcija Titograda je Duklja, na tri kilometra od grada. Ovo naselje je podignuto za vreme rimskog cara Dioklecijana, na mestu gde se Zeta uliva u Moraču. Do danas su očuvani temelji mnogih zgrada, izvesni fragmenti, skulpture i niz interesantnih predmeta umetničkih zanata.

22   Iz članka *Pruga Beograd–Bar*

iz časopisa *Revija*

Pruga "Beograd–Bar", koja najkraćim putem spaja gotovo polovinu Jugoslavije (49 odsto teritorije sa devet i po miliona stanovnika) sa Jadranskim morem, a to znači sa svetom, svetskim tržištem i svetskom naučnom i tehničkom revolucijom, spada u izuzetne poduhvate ne samo u Jugoslaviji nego i u Evropi. Prolazi kroz najlepše i dosad nepristupačne predele zemlje, kroz dvesta pedeset i tri tunela, preko stotinu mostova, što znači stotinu dubokih, divljih i vanredno lepih kanjona (most preko Male reke visok je dvesta metara) u ukupnoj dužini preko četrnaest kilometara, da bi na domak mora isplovila između planinskih masiva Durmitora i Prokletija na visini od hiljadu trideset i šest metara, a zatim se naglo — kao orao u kružnom sletanju — spustila na svega trideset metara nadmorske visine. I u jednom zamahu projurila preko Skadarskog jezera, u čijoj drevnoj tišini pelikani legu svoje mlade, i zaustavila se na najlepšoj i najsunčanijoj obali Jadranskog mora.

23 Iz romana *Mirisi, zlato i tamjan*

SLOBODAN NOVAK

Dragu sam ugledao na istom onom mjestu na kojem sam je bio ostavio prije toliko dana. Stajala je na palubi pokraj onoga stvarno prekrasnog kofera, kao da je upravo izašla iz tramvaja i zastala trenutak na stanici pod kestenovima. Mislim da je taj kofer najljepša i najskupocjenija stvar koju imamo. Predmet. A zašto imamo baš kofer tako sjajan i fin, bogzna! Gotovo ga i ne upotrebljavamo, a tolike druge stvari čovjek nema, mili bože! Draga je takva žena, da bi morala imati sve svoje u stilu kofera, i još preko toga tušta i tma raznih stvarčica i predmeta i tri tovara blaga. Nema na cijeloj palubi osobe tako skladne, i ne bi je takve ni bilo da je uplovila sama pokojna ,,*Queen Mary*'' Ah, šta ćemo, znam ja, ne vrijedi govoriti!

Draga i ja nismo se javljali jedno drugome onako kako se to radi, preko glava svih ljudi, mahanjem, istezanjem vrata, propinjanjem na prste. Nasmiješili smo se samo jedno drugome, i ja sam, istina, pošao onamo do samog broda pod palubu na kojoj je stajala, a nisam htio čekati podno skale. Gledao sam je odozdo, hajde de, a ona se znala svakako ukusno držati, pritisnula je koljenima suknju o brodsku ogradu i pitala u onom metežu otprilike: »kako gore?«, i ja sam glavom i ramenima rekao da je sve uglavnom dobro, i htio sam odmah pitati sada nju kako je gore, jer i Zagreb je gore kao i Madonina kuća, i za nas je uvijek sve negdje gore, ali sam valjda učinio nesuvislu kretnju, pa je Draga samo klimnula glavom, misleći da onako nešto izvodim bez veze radi ove usrane publike oko nas, koja uvijek očekuje da ljudi s broda na obalu i obrnuto ubrzano nešto dojavljuju jedni drugima kao da je smak svijeta. Učinila mi se ipak malo zagonetna, i ponovio sam nekoliko puta uzastopce obrvama znakove pitanja, ali ona je na to odgovorila kao: »Nema problema, zašto ne, izvolite, samo ubijte!«, pa se začas opet smijuljila, onako sa sjenama oko usta i preko nosa, i budući da nisam poznavao svoju ženu, jer žene se ne mogu upoznati, pomirio sam se da pričekam miris njene kože, po kojemu obično najbolje zaključujem. K meni je silazila skalom moja zlatna konzerva s koje je otpala etiketa, i ja sam svestrano gladan samo čekao koje i kakove sokove da izlučim kad bude deklariran sadržaj.

— Kako je? — velim ja i ljubim je u obraz i uzimam kofer. — Djeca dobro, svi dobro?

Ona je samo potvrdila mumljanjem. Mirisala je po daljinama koje se prostiru između jutrošnjeg izlaska sunca i ovoga podneva. A od ličnih mirisa nisam mogao osjetiti ništa u ovom konvencionalnom dodiru pred brodskom i obalskom posadom i pred građanima grada.

Iskopali smo se iz toga grozda podno skale i ušli u malu povorku što se napuštajući pristanište kretala ispod zidina gradskih i teglila cijeli jedan dućan artikala koji se ne mogu naći na otočkim tezgama. Draga je imala nekakav izlomljen, usporeni korak kao dugonoge ptice močvarne, i o svemu je pričala napola, ali prilično zadovoljna, iako je gore navodno sve nekako drugačije; i sve su konvencionalnosti bile u redu — pozdravi, zdravlje, poruke i drugo, i onda je na kraju rekla da neka požurimo kako ne bi Erminija čekala. Rekao sam de nema Erminije kod nas, da Madona zna za moj izlazak, i stao joj podastirati kratku skicu našeg budućeg stila življenja i djelomične emancipacije, ali ona je od početka ubrzala korak pomalo panično, i nije se dala urazumiti, i nije se više putem do kuće moglo s njom išta ozbiljno načeti. Samo mi je žureći stepenicama prema pjaceti zadihano predbacila:

— Nisi mi smio to učiniti. Ako ti je bilo teško, morao si mi reći, i ne bih nikud odlazila. Kako to sada izgleda da je ona u kući sama!

— Vrlo važno! Neće ništa ukrasti! — ljutito sam se otresao vukući onaj kofer žustrim tempom uza strmenice i stubišta. — Čega se toliko bojiš? Neće pobjeći na groblje!

Ona, međutim, nije odgovorila i nije se više ni osvrtala na mene, nego je, malo bočno, kao da se skriva, gotovo ljupko zajedrila uza zidove prema kući.

Kada sam stigao za njom, ona je već bila ogrnuta kućnom haljinom. Bila je u žurbi isprva zaboravila šešir, onda skine i njega, premda se on, mislim, skida prvi. Malo rašešuri svoju krutu trajnu i uđe u Madoninu sobu govoreći sasvim obično i smireno:

— Kako vam je jutros? Rekli su mi da ste me zvali. Treba li vam mlakoga čaja malo, ha?

Madona je šutjela. Šutjela, šutjela.

Draga ju je zbunila svojim mirom, ali nije bilo jasno je li i pobijedila. Još je malo poslovala oko komode, i onda izašla iz sobe isto tako posleno kako je bila ušla. Izišavši pokrila je upaničeno dlanovima usta i stala kolutati očima, pitajući se šta će biti. Zatim se prihvatila kuhanja, jer je vrijeme ručku već i prošlo, a ja sam danas špekulirao s novom kuharicom, pa sam samo sve priredio, vatru naložio i — ogladnio.

Pitao sam je već nekoliko puta kako je gore, to me je neizrecivo zanimalo, ali nikako da dobijem prava odgovora, ili barem kakav zalogajčić, radi orijentacije, ili da se nasladim. Zato sam joj se primakao s leđa i zaprijetio da ću joj glavu odrubiti ako ne odgovori na tri pitanja koja glase sva tri: Kako gore?!

One se na to stresla od neke jeze i ne odvraćajući očiju sa svog posla rekla najprije zbunjeno:

— Ne znam. Sve je nekako drukčije — onda se malo zamislila, pa me postrance pogledala i naoko vedrije rekla — Drugačije nekako, zbilja. Sve je drugačije — kao da je željela učiniti ležernijom svoju prvu toliko ozbiljnu riječ.

Čudio sam se, kako to drugačije. Nekako?! Šta znači drugačije? Od čega drugačije? Drugačije nego prije? Drugačije nego što je ona zamišljala da će biti? Šta znači drugačije?

— I ti sama si drugačija!

— Pa da. I ja.

24   Iz romana *Raspust*

ALEKSANDAR VUČO

Krajem juna, kad smo dobili ocene i obojica znali da smo prešli u VI razred, pozvao me Ladislav na užinu. Stan im se nalazio u centralnoj zgradi u nekoj vrsti četvorougaonog tornja koji je strčao iznad bolničkih paviljona. Zagladio sam kosu i zazvonio. U malom polumračnom predsoblju vise na čiviluku bele oficirske bluze iznesene da se prenu iz zimskog sna. Prekoputa, ovalno ogledalo u teškom pozlaćenom ramu. Miris karbola. Ladislav se pojavio uznemiren, pomalo postiđen. Otvorio je jedna od četvora vrata i pokazao mi rukom da uđem. (gest koji je zastao između preterane učtivosti i drugarske kordijalnosti). Ušao sam u prostranu sobu. Spuštene roletne štite je od sunca, na pola puta od zenita do zalaska. Zidovi tamni, prevučeni ljubičastim tapetima. Slike i fotografije. Nameštaj sakriven pod teškim stolnjacima, prekrivačima, izvezenim miljeima, navlakama.

Na sredini sobe stajala je njegova majka. Sitna, vrlo uskog lica. Njena začešljana proseda kosa zadržala je gipkost života. Rasejani refleks njene ruke kad se sa mnom rukovala. Na somotskoj pantljici oko vrata kamea u zlatnom okviru. Beli venecijanski šal prebačen preko uskih ramena. Skrivena prsa. Lik koji se sreće u knjigama.

Nasmejala se na mene plavim pogledom, malo prepredenim, i rekla brzo skandirajući reči:

— Baš sam čitala Voltera. Zamislite, deco, zabranjivao je šetnje, smanjivao ljudima obroke . . . Aaa! vi ste taj Dragan o kome mi je Ladislav toliko pričao. Stanite, molim vas, pored njega. Hajde! Lađo, molim te i ti, samo za trenutak. Da vidim nešto . . .

Uzela nas je za ruke, dovela na sredinu sobe i sastavila nam leđa.

— Viši ste od mog Lađe za dva santimetra. Ko bi rekao! Ali on je zato širi . . . širi u ramenima. Eto, pogledajte u ogledalu, uverite se sami. I to još koliko! rekla je s neprikrivenim likovanjem. Gotovo pakosno.

Približila nas zatim prozoru:

— Vaše su oči svetlije, šarene. Njegove ugasite, na tatu. I mnogo dublje, mnogo dublje . . . Lepi moj Ladislave!

Seli smo u fotelje sa širokim naslonima, oko okruglog stola pretrpanog kutijicama sa inkrustacijama od sedefa i porodičnim albumima ukoričenim u somot, sa upadljivo velikim srmenim zatvaračima. Trajalo je to samo nekoliko minuta. S bukom nestašnog deteta skočila je, prišla klaviru, podigla poklopac:

— Volite li muziku? — i zasvirala Šopenovu mazurku.

Ostavljala je na mene utisak kao da je pijana ili gola.

Prestala je da svira. Okrenula se:

— Znate, ja sam Poljkinja, otac mi je bio fabrikant sirćeta ili kvasca, ne znam više tačno čega . . . Nije bilo onda bogataša u Varšavi koji me nije prosio. Ali, zašto vam to pričam? A da . . . vuklo me nešto da provodim dvostruki život, stepenice koje odvode dalje, više nego što je sudbina odredila. Devojački snovi? Zinite da vam kažem! Udala sam se za oficira — protiv očeve volje. Bio je strašan tata-Tadija. Pobegla sam s Milivojem. On je onda bio u vojnoj deputaciji, lep kao sveti Đorđe. Bili smo dugo srećni. I . . .

Talasi rumenila smenjivali su se s bledilom na Lađinom licu.

— Izvini, mama, ali Dragana to ne interesuje, rekao je odlučno. Dozvoli da mu pokažem fotografije.

Pošli smo duž zidova. Ona je, uvređena, nastavila Šopena.

U tankim ramovima: konji. Pastuvi za priplod, ždrebne kobile, serija prvih na derbiju u Epsomu za poslednjih deset godina, steeplechase-ovi, kolekcije džokeja, fotografije malih i mršavih ljudi s posvetama i potpisima, diplome sa pečatima, treneri, hipodromi, štale, pedigriji. Na policama u levom uglu: potkovice (jedna od zlata), mamuze, džokejske ešarpe, ukrštani korbači; prekoputa slike oficira; vesele grupe na izletima, manevri, terenska jahanja, kapetanske zvezdice, pijanke. Na jednom zidu, sasvim sâm, veliki portret u boji — njen Milovoje. Prav, modrocrnih očiju, sabljastih obrva.

Bio sam zapanjen. Sve zajedno navaljivalo je na mene teret simboličnih sugestija, sa izuzetno mračnom snagom, raskošnom i nesnosnom na putu osvajanja mog duha.

U sobu je ušla mlada devojka, možda godinu-dve starija od mene. Crna suknja do člankova utegnutih u duboke crne cipele na šnir. Oko struka, tankog kao u osice, širok kaiš od crnog laka. Bela bluza kroja muške košulje. Bezdano crne pletenice oko potiljka, oštar rez razdeljka na sredini. Oči ni zelene ni plave. Iz njih bujaju dugačke, izvijene trepavice. Obrazi od tamnog voska.

— Možete da pređete u trpezariju, obratila se svima u sobi, užina je servirana.

— Da te pretstavim, povukao me za ruku Ladislav. — Vanda, moja sestra — Dragan, moj najbolji drug.

— Dakle, to ste vi, rekla je glasom u kome je plovilo nešto čudno i tamno, a ja sam mislila . . .

— Šta si mislila? zapitao je Ladislav veselo.

— Da je tvoj prijatelj drukčiji . . .

Okrenula se i pošla prema vratima trpezarije.

Majka je još jednako svirala, dajući nam glavom znak da ne treba da čekamo na nju.

Pili smo čokoladu, jeli sutlijaš naprašen cimetom, i neke kolačice u obliku mnogokrakih zvezda, natopljene medom i mirisom vanile. Osetio sam ponovo da nešto tamno, čudno, uznemirujuće lebdi oko Vande i moli za uzajamnost. Pričala nam je o mačkici, prljavoj, još slepoj, koju je našla pred jednim podrumskim prozorom. »Mici! Mici!« zvala je, sagla se, i podigla s poda crno mače. S njim u ruci ustala je i zapitala me iznenadno:

— Dakle, iduće godine u ovo doba i vi u Akademiju? Konjica ili artilerija?

Odgovorio sam da bih mnogo voleo, ali da sumnjam da će mi otac dozvoliti.

— Od rođenja me sprema za trgovca. Treba da nasledim njegovu izvozničku radnju, dodao sam zasipajući gorkom ironijom svaku reč.

Stavila je mače na rame, oborila guste trepavice i rekla nešto kao da se vidi da mi je na usnama ostalo još malo majčinog mleka, i da to treba da obrišem što pre, jer moj život pripada samo meni.

— Vanda! — opomenuo ju je Ladislav.

Zatresla je prkosno glavom i prišla otvorenom prozoru u dnu sobe.

Ljubičasta svetlost je ležala na stvarima, na njenoj kosi, na krovovima bolničkih paviljona. Kao nanos sveže boje. U topolama razbijeno ogledalo zalazećeg sunca.

Vratila se i sela ponovo za sto. Njeno telo se razvijalo, toplo, savitljivo. Nije mogla da mi se približi a da ne zadrhtim. Uzimala je maha u meni. Zavladala je mojim mislima.

— Treba da budete energični. Recite ocu da je u pitanju život ili smrt. Da sam ja slušala tatu i mamu, danas bih pevala solfedo u muzičkoj školi. Vaspitajmo roditelje!

25 Iz pripovijetke *Rođendan*

ANTUN ŠOLJAN

Bili smo ovdje davno prije, i obećali smo da ćemo se vratiti. Nitko nije ispunio obećanje, kao ni hiljadu drugih obećanja danih u zanosu, zaboravljenih u slijedećem ravnodušnom trenutku. Obećanja za koja je uvijek prekasno. Uvijek smo se ponosili time što ih ne održavamo, i što promjenljivi živimo u promjenljivom svijetu.

Nitko nikad nije zažalio što se nemamo kamo vratiti.

Kuću je pronašao Marijan, prijatelj moje mladosti, o kojem još ni danas ne mogu misliti sasvim bez uzbuđenja. Bio je skitnica i lutalac, slobodan i ciničan na jeziku i u postupcima, prema ničemu nije pokazivao poštovanja, ništa nije volio više od sebe, ništa ga nije vezalo. Bježao je od svakog jarma koji bi mu svijet pokušao naturiti. Izbjegavao je rodbinske odnose, dugoročne poslovne ugovore, stalne prijatelje i trajne ljubavnice. Uvijek je radije prihvaćao više nesigurnih žena nego jednu sigurnu. Uvijek je radije putovao, povlačio se po vlakovima i brodovima, nego što je stanovao u određenom gradu, u vlastitom stanu. Mrzio je stvari koje su u njemu budile želju da ih posjeduje.

Rijetko smo se viđali, ali naši su susreti, u raznim mjestima i u neočekivanim okolnostima, uvijek bili ispunjeni nekim mističnim značenjem i za jednog i za drugog. U njima je uvijek bilo neke težine, nekog prazničkog, svečanog osjećanja, kao da se dešava nešto izvanredno, nešto što će imati dalekosežne posljedice ne samo za naš život nego i za sve ljude oko nas, ali, izvana, ti su sastanci izgledali savršeno prirodno, logično i svakodnevno. Bili smo, čini mi se, kao dva istraživača koji se posve neočekivano susretnu u džungli centralne Afrike, pozdrave se normalno i civilizirano, kao da su se tek jučer rastali na ulicama rodnog grada i, smatrajući ovaj svoj susret jednako običnim i normalnim, ćaskaju izvjesno vrijeme o posve nevažnim stvarima, a onda se opet, bez mnogo ceremonija, izgube svaki u svom pravcu među lijane i tamne močvarne biljke debelog lišća.

Marijan je, u vrijeme o kojem govorim, neprestano lutao po obali i otocima. Meni je ta njegova skitnja izgledala potpuno besmislena i besciljna, ali vrlo je vjerojatno da su drugima isto tako izgledala nemirna i stalna traženja moje mladosti, unatoč tome ispunjena unutarnjom logikom, vođena jednom nejasnom zvijezdom koju sam samo ja naslućivao.

Otkrio je zaboravljenu kuću na zapuštenom otoku, i tako se desilo da smo on, ja i dvije sada već bezimene djevojke otišli na petnaestodnevno praznikovanje negdje u kasno toplo proljeće one zaboravljene godine kad sam proživio možda najsretnije trenutke svoga života.

Stigli smo naveče na otok i naselili se u kuću u potpunom mraku — nije bilo ni elektrike, ni vode, ni zahoda. Kuća je tada još bila u koliko-toliko pristojnom stanju: imala je dvije sobe i kuhinju s ogromnim starinskim kaminom, i kad smo prikupili razbacane crvotočne dijelove namještaja, izvlačeći ga ispod naslaga prašine, uspjeli smo skucati dva staromodna bračna kreveta, komodu bez ladica, stol i nekoliko klimavih izjedenih stolica. To su bili jedini ostaci bivših vlasnika, kojima nikad nismo ustanovili identitet.

Nekoliko sati lupali smo po kući, u oblacima prašine, ubijali skorpione, zavirivali u mračne uglove pri titravom sablasnom svjetlu voštanih svijeća. Prostrli smo gumene patent-madrace na krevete, osposobili smo ulazna vrata usadivši ih na zarđale šarke, i odredili smo u kamenjaru mjesto za noćne potrebe, s čvrstom odlukom da sutra iskopamo pravu pravcatu jamu.

Čovjeku tako malo treba za sreću.

S druge strane otoka upravo te godine stari samostan pretvarao se u hotel. Hotel još nije radio, ali kako su već bili dovezli kojekakvih stvari, u njemu se nastanio čuvar sa ženom — jedini ljudi na otoku osim nas. Čuvarova žena dopustila nam je da skuhamo večeru na njenoj vatri i u njenom posuđu. Zgražala se kako možemo stanovati u onakvom ćumezu, i žalila „ovako zgodne djevojke". Njeno nam je zgražanje neizmjerno laskalo. Marijan i ja ostavili smo, naravno, djevojke da se bave priređivanjem večere, i one su otišle, dvije zvonolike sjene, po srebrnastoj mjesečini otoka, spotičući se o blistavo kamenje, uživajući u novim ulogama, smijući se zvonkim, visokim, sretnim smijehom koji je odjekivao u praznim nebesima.

Marijan i ja smo obišli kuću, gazdinski je tapšući po zidovima i dovracima, a onda smo sjeli za stol u mračnoj kuhinji, upalili dvije voštanice i zaigrali malu partiju karata udvoje. Igrali smo u sitne novce, tek toliko da ne bude džabe, neku nevinu penzionersku igru na gruboj neobojenoj dasci stola, nabacujući se dosjetkama, budalaštinama i ludorijama više nego kartama, zadovoljni gubitkom i dobitkom, i sami sobom. Svijeće su treperile toplo i praznički kao u stara vremena.

— Ho, ho, ho! — uživao je Marijan. — Ovako su živjeli naši preci. Uglavnom nisu ništa vidjeli. Opet sam zamijenio asa herc za asa karo.

— Baš je perfektno — rekao sam.

— Dobro je kao što može biti — rekao je Marijan.

— Nemaš pojma o igri — optužio sam ga. — Nemoj se ispričavati svjetlom.

— Sa ovakvima igram i po mraku. Da nam je još samo malo vina bilo bi božanstveno.

— Gdje nam je bila glava? Znali smo da idemo u pustinju. Trebaloj e da ponesemo pića. Boca vina, knjiga pjesama i žena, što bi rekao Omar. Trebalo je misliti.

I u taj čas, bez kucanja, bez ikakvog prethodnog upozorenja, sa škripom i sporo, kao sama od sebe, otvorila su se vrata. Otvorila su se širom, dostojanstveno, i na pragu, uokviren mrakom, titrav i sablastan od svijeća, pojavio se jedan nezemaljski starac u crnom odijelu, sjedokos i uspravan kao kralj duhova. Pogledao nas je bez riječi, polako, jednog pa drugog, držeći u rukama dvije tamne boce, ne mičući se s mjesta, ogromna noćna ptica.

Mi smo sjedili u žutom krugu svijeća, odjednom sitni i beznačajni prema vanjskom svijetu, beskrajnoj noći iz koje se, evo, svakog časa mogu pojaviti neviđene sablasti i donijeti nam neočekivano. Sjedili smo, ne ispuštajući iz ruku karte, jedini kontakt s realnošću, i okrenuli se samo glavama prema svečanom starcu, čekajući poruku s nekog drugog svijeta, nepoznatog i možda strašnog. Osjećali smo se kao da nas je pronašao kurir same sudbine.

Starac nas je promotrio bez ijedne riječi, a zatim dostojanstveno i polako iskoračio iz nejasnog polumraka na vratima, prišao stolu i stavio pažljivo, među svijeće, dvije čvrsto začepljene tamne trbušaste boce. Još jednom nas je bezizražajno pogledao, okrenuo se ravnomjerno kao robot i otišao, sporo i pažljivo zatvorivši iza sebe vrata. U trenutku kad je stavljao boce na stol zapamtio sam mu oči: bile su nebeski plave, prazne i mirne.

Sjedili smo još nekoliko trenutaka nepokretno, ne snalazeći se, a onda smo prasnuli u čudesan smijeh, koji nas nije napuštao cijelog tog divnog praznikovanja, i otvorili smo boce iz kojih je zaklokotalo gusto crveno vino, iskričavo i mirisavo, sunčano i pitko, vino istiješteno iz grozdova zvijezda.

Popili smo nekoliko čaša svečano kao da se pričešćujemo, a zatim nekoliko gurmanski, ocjenjujući aromu, boju, temperaturu. I uskoro smo se prestali iščuđavati kako je i odakle je došlo, pa smo nastavili kartati pomalo, pomalo pijuckati, i napili smo se kao Rusi, uz tople svijeće, i počeli pjevati bacajući karte nasumce po stolu, pjevati tako srdačno i tako glasno da je cijela stara kuća odjekivala iznutra kao pijana bačva, odjednom opet puna života, preporođena.

Kasnije su došle djevojke s hranom, i vidjevši nas sretne postale su i same sretne, i napile se zajedno s nama, pjevale s nama, u staroj napuštenoj kući na kraju svijeta, u malom žutom krugu toplog svjetla usred ogromne noći.

Djevojke su nam objasnile da je onaj starac u stvari čuvar hotela, nijem od rođenja, i da su ga one poslale plativši vino. Ali, iako plaćena, sreća je ipak sreća.

26 Iz članka *Njegovo veličanstvo—kiosk za novine*

iz časopisa *Revija*

Po književniku Albertu Kamiju, današnji čovek je pre svega "gutač novina". Ovu bolest XX veka nisu uspeli da izbegnu ni Jugosloveni koji od listova očekuju sve: istinu, informaciju, zabavu, razbibrigu i na kraju — dobar materijal za čišćenje prozora.

No, na vidiku se pojavljuje najljući neprijatelj svakog lista — televizija! Koncem pedesetih godina rađa se u Jugoslaviji jedan novi, do tada nepoznati medijum — žurnalistika pokretnih slika. Od njegove pojave do danas, novine i filmovi morali su da prođu kroz mnoga iskušenja, bez ikakve svetlije perspektive pred sobom. Bitka postaje sve ogorčenija! Neki listovi propadaju, a oni drugi, koji žele da opstanu, prinuđeni su da odbace svoju iznošenu sivu garderobu i pređu na obojene tiraže. Tako se rađa nekoliko šarenih ilustrovanih listova. Ima i različitih filmskih žurnala, koji, zahvaljujući svojoj atraktivnoj materiji imaju veoma veliki broj čitalaca. Listovi koji su se do tada morali vezivati za film, opisujući navike i skandale čuvenih starova, počinju iznenada da se vezuju uz televiziju, donoseći najpre informacije o programu, a docnije čak i najsitnije intrige i dogodovštine iz sveta s one strane ekrana.

Potrošačka publika postaje sve razmaženija. Ona traži da bude zabavljena i da joj se list udvara. Ona više ne može da podnese oskudnost, stereotipan način izražavanja, loš kvalitet hartije i bledu fotografiju. One hoće najbolje od najboljeg, inače se uopšte ne pojavljuje pred svojim kioskom, već pritiskom prsta na dugme otvara prostore televizijskog pejzaža, koji daleko više nudi za daleko manje novaca.

27 Iz članka *Kada se temelji tresu*

iz časopisa *Revija*

Kuća se ničim ne izdvaja od ostalih. Ali iz njenih temelja vibrira ritam. To je jedan od mnogobrojnih beogradskih disko-klubova. Sve ih je više u svim gradovima. I u mnogim selima. Mladi svet ih je prihvatio i oni su postali deo svakodnevnog života. Te mračne podrumske prostorije u kojima vlada zaglušujuća buka, gde se neprestano smenjuju jarki svetlosni efekti, gde je svako sâm i svi su sa svima. U disko-klubovima nema stare, lepe romantike, zaljubljenih parova, laganih melodija. Cela prostorija podrhtava od zvuka, svetla i pokreta. Stare, klasične igranke gube publiku. Na njih je trebalo ići u parovima, u svečanim odelima. U diskoklubove mladići i devojke mogu da odu sami, u starim farmerkama, da ostanu sami i da se ne osete usamljeni.

Mladi ne traže mnogo — najvažnija je dobra muzika i društvo vršnjaka. To je atmosfera u kojoj se dobro osećaju i u koju se rado vraćaju.

28 Iz romana *Proljeća Ivana Galeba*

VLADAN DESNICA

Danas je nebo osvanulo zastrto. Tek sredinom jutra pojavilo se sunce i dovabilo me na prozor, kao guštera. Prekinuo sam pisanje i stajao iza stakla gledajući u uski prostor s nasadima između dva paviljona. Najednom zatutnji automobil i ustavi se pred ulazom u zgradu. Crn, ulašten, ispupčen krov sjajio se na suncu. Iz automobila ispade čitava mala familija: otac, majka, kćerka, već djevojka, i sinčić. Zacijelo su došli nekome u pohode. Otac je zalupio stražnja vrata ne propustivši da prije toga malo spusti staklo, radi ventilacije, kako kasnije ne bi bilo sparno. Zatim je izvadio iz džepa zveckavi snopić ključica i malim plosnatim mjedenim *yale*-om brižno zaključao. Za prednja vrata nije pokazao podjednaku očinsku brigu; njih je samo zalupio. Prošli su stubištem, malčice bučnije nego posjetioci-pješaci, a zatim su se čuli njihovi koraci na hodniku, sve dok nisu zamakli u sobu mog susjeda. Vrata koja su se za njima zatvorila presjekla su mome uhu povišene glasove iznenađenja i pozdravljanja kod susreta.

Dječak se kratko zadržao u sobi. Zamišljam da se i za to vrijeme premetao s noge na nogu i u sebi brojio do stotinu, ili do trista, koliko je već unaprijed sebi odredio da mora najmanje ostati kod bolesnika. A onda se iskrao i sišao opet k prijatelju automobilu. Očevidno, sasvim skorašnja nabavka. Izvadio je ispod prednjeg sjedišta veliku novu krpu jelenje kože i uzeo brisati staklo, blistavi metal hladnjaka, farove. Tad je sjeo za volan (vidio sam ga iskosa, kroz obrisano staklo pod niskim krovom), i stao naizmjence upirati nogama u pedale, uvlašno kretati amo tamo volan, onako »na suho«; pritom je skupio usne: upotpunjavao je iluziju imitirajući šum motora. Zatim je stavio u pogon brisač, koji se okretao desno-lijevo, desno-

lijevo, malko zapinjući po suhom staklu, jer danas, eto, nažalost
kiše ni za lijek! Baš su nesretna djeca! Nikad da im potrefi ono
što bi u taj čas trebalo!

A gore u sobi međutim su torokali. Postavljali bolesniku
pitanja o njemu, o njegovom zdravlju, pa mu ne davali vremena
da odgovori već novim pitanjima presijecali njegove tek zapo-
čete odgovore, upadali jedno drugom u riječ i jedno drugo
nadglasavali ... U njihovom se čavrljanju, svakako, bar
desetak puta navraćala riječ »kola«, »naša kola«, u raznim
spregama, kao kod vježba u padežima. Vidjeli su da je lijep dan,
pa su pomislili: zašto da ne iskoristimo pa trknemo našim
kolima da ga posjetimo? Doduše, put nije najbolji, ali kola su
nova, imaju dobre amortizere, pa hvala bogu! vozit ćemo nešto
polaganije! I tako, posjedali su u kola, Viktor je sjeo za volan,
pripalio cigaru, i cigara još nije ni dogorjela, a već su bili tu ...
Ali gdje je Zvonko? Uvijek on nekud šmigne! No, sigurno je
dolje, kod kola ... Samo zaboga, da ne bi što taknuo! ... Ali
ne će, ne će, bez brige, razuman je on, u tim stvarima ...
Bože moj, treba shvatiti, njega to jako zanima, na koncu konca,
dijete je, svi smo bili djeca ... i tu se razdragana lica kolektivno
obraćaju bolesniku za potvrdu i uviđavnost ...

Ali sad zbilja već moraju da krenu, dugo su se zadržali.
Viktor naime ima da obavi još jedan mali poslić prije ručka,
samo, ne znadu — zna li to možda bolesnik? — ne, nažalost
ni bolesnik to ne zna, — ne bi li im bilo bolje da na povratku
krenu gornjim putem? Zašto da se vraćaju istim putem kad
mogu ... ali ne, ne, nema smisla, gornji je put doduše nešto
kraći, ali zašto riskirati, ta i onako, s našim kolima, to znači
svega par minuta razlike, a to ne igra nikakvu ulogu, nema
zaista nikakva smisla štrapacirati kola. Uostalom, donji put
kojim su došli ipak je uglavnom pristojan, i zašto bi sad
riskirali ... a baš im je drago što bolesnik tako dobro izgleda,
vjerujte, čisto dobro, raduju se, i nadaju se da će uskoro,
sasvim uskoro, itakodalje ... He, dakle, još jednom, drago im
je, raduju se, od sveg srca se raduju, ustaju, zakopčavaju

ogrtače, baš se raduju, baš zakopčavaju ogrtače, karirane putne ogrtače od *tweeda*, i nadaju se da će uskoro. . . oh bože! gotovo su zaboravili, donijeli su cvijeće, malo gladiola, krasnih, svježih gladiola, naslonili su ih tamo na radiator . . . o, hvala, hvala . . . i nadaju se da će uskoro, sasvim uskoro . . . hvala . . . he, dakle doviđenja, do skorog viđenja, hvala, hvala, još jednom doviđenja! — I konačno odlaze.

Promiču opet hodnikom, silaze stepenicama, dobrostivo se osmjehuju vrataru. Viktor vadi iz džepa mali zveckavi svjetlucavi snopić, izabire plosnati mjedeni ključić, brižno ga uvlači u bravicu, otključava stražnja vratašca, spušta još malo niže staklo. A Zvonko zbilja nije lijepo učinio, što će samo reći bolesnik, kakvo će mišljenje imati o njemu. A baš je lijep dan, i dobro je što su iskoristili, jer za sutra se već ne zna, za sutra se nikad baš sasvim sigurno ne zna! . . . A srećom nema mnogo prašine . . . A njoj bolesnik zbilja nije napravio tako loš dojam. Ni njemu, ni njemu, on je očekivao gore, mnogo gore. Smještaju se u kola. Viktor sjeda za volan, pripaljuje novu cigaru, namješta zeleni šeširić, zeleni šeširić s runolistom, uvlači u kola i posljednju nogu. Zvonko sjeda pored njega. Pleuritično kašljucnu zalupnuta vrata — i kola kreću.

29

Iz romana *Kiklop*

RANKO MARINKOVIĆ

Visoko gore na krovu palače razvio platno kad je pao mrak i stao da se dere — MAAR-CENTROREKLAM! Kad je ispisao po platnu tajanstvenim svjetlom svoje moćno ime, MAAROVA slova izvedu luckasti divertisman pjevajući unisono neku pjesmu u slavu svoga gospodara. Odskakuću zatim u zamračeno nebo, a on još jednom vikne zadivljenom svijetu MAAR-TONFILMSKA REKLAMA.

Pojavi se zatim kuća jadna i prljava, naherena krova, izvaljenih vrata, a iz njenih prozora u paničnom strahu iskaču zgužvane i musave košulje, sablasna torza bez glave i nogu. Uz muziku dance macabra vuku se bolesne žrtve nečistoće prema kotlu na vatri u kome nestrpljivo kupi gusta bijela pjena. S usidjeličkim nepovjerenjem, oklijevajući još na samom rublu kotla (boje se da ih ne nasamare) skaču košulje u pjenu . . . i gle, nepovjerenje je bilo posljedica glupe predrasude, jer evo kako jedna za drugom blistavobijele izlaze iz kotla i marširajući u redu pjevaju oduševljeno ,,Radion pere sâm". — Onda se na platnu pojavila sfinga i pita gledaoce dalekim pustinjskim glasom: ,,Je li to moguće?" i odmah lijepa daktilografkinja pokazuje kako nije moguće istovremeno pisati na dvije mašine. ,,A je li ovo moguće?" pita sfinga. — Ne, ni to nije moguće . . . da voda teče uzbrdo. Pa ni to nije moguće, da se kuća gradi od krova, ni to da se Sunce okreće oko Zemlje . . . ,,ali je zato moguće da ,,Tungsram Crypton" sijalice sa dvaput spiraliziranom niti daju dvostruko jače svjetlo uz isti potrošak struje" . . . i zasja na platnu sijalica kao sunce nebesko te je valjalo i zažmiriti od strašnoga sjaja. — Tada na platno dopleše nestašna djevojčica u piknjastoj dinderlici i izdeklamira djevičanskim glasom internatkinje kod časnih sestara: „Sjajno pere sapun Zora, to se zbilja mora priznat . . . priznat mora", popravlja grešku, uzaludno, gledaoci se smiju. Djevojčica se povlači postiđeno. Iza djevojčice slijedi putnik, vuče dva teška kovčega, a iza njega vijuga cesta u beskrajnoj perspektivi. Odozgo putnika sunce bije vatrenim bičevima, no on korača lako i veselo, i namigujući lukavo došaptava publici u povjerenju: „Sa „Palma" potpeticama prelazite dug put bez ikakva umora" i pokazuje ogromne tabane: — doista, „Palma" potpetice! . . . „Kastner i Öhler", najveća robna kuća na Balkanu, prosula iz roga svog obilja nevjerojatne i čarobne stvari „od igle do kamiona", a mašta gledalaca kljuca, kljuca po tim raskošima. — Julijo Meini sve hoće da napoji kitajskim, ceylonskim čak i ruskim čajem, a od kava — samo kava „Haag", jer ona štedi vaše srce. — Kihni ako možeš nakon „Bayerova" aspirina! Dok ti spavaš, „Darmol" radi, a „Planinka" čaj ima patriotsku dužnost da čisti arijevsku krv. „Elida" krema strepi za tvoj teint. „Interkozma" se kune da će za najkraće vrijeme pošumiti tvoju ogoljelu glavu. „Kalodont" je ljuti neprijatelj zubnoga kamenca, a „Vi-Ha-Ge" vas vragoljanski pita jeste li muškarac? I na koncu — „Prvi hrvatski zavod za sjajne pogrebe" uz najveće poštovanje slobodan je da vas podsjeti na vaše dostojanstvo pa . . . izvolite pogledati: crno lakirana kola s baroknim zlatnim anđelima, konji sjajne crne dlake, udoban kovčeg, pratnja uzorno trijeznog osoblja s admiralskim kapama, te je tako vaša smrt još jedan uspjeh i ljepota, gotovo poetična . . .

30

Iz eseja *O Kranjčevićevoj lirici*

MIROSLAV KRLEŽA

On je izrastao u vremenu pred konac prošlog stoljeća, kada se čitavo jedno vrijeme, u evropskom mjerilu, izgubilo u neukusu malograđanske pseudoromantike, i čitava njegova pomodna faktura povezana je neodvojivo upravo s tom malograđanskom pseudoromantikom. Retuš njegovih slika i alegorija poslastičarski je sladak, jer su ljepote te pseudoromantike bile slatke kao poslastičarska caklina. Aranžman njegovih kompozicija je melodramatski banalan, kao sve što se komponiralo osamdesetih godina. Rasvjeta njegova je teatralna. On radi s najglasnijim romantičnim sredstvom kontrastiranja: elegično uprljano cinizmom, baladeskno i tragično svladano sarkazmom, pseudoromantično lijepo i dobro u sudaru s luciferskim demonizmom zla i rugobe. Sve su njegove elegične slike dekorativno uokvirene nadzemaljskim simbolima i on je uvijek na granici kiča, kao što su to svi žanr-drvorezi devedesetih godina, koje je kao urednik »Nade« tako rado i obilato štampao. I sredina u kojoj je živio, i vrijeme u kome je pisao, i uzori u koje je gledao kao u domaće književne autoritete, i književno-pomodna sredstva koja je upotrebljavao kod svoga izražavanja, sve mu je to kod stvaranja više odmagalo nego pomagalo i više smetalo nego pogodovalo. Pa ipak: ispod ove vanjske vještačke naprave, ispod ovog neukusnog i banalnog književnog steznika, pod tom površnom pseudoromantičnom korom javlja se njegovo unutarnje lice i osjeća se njegovo krvavo tijelo, prodire elemenat njegove lične, individualne, kranjčevićevske snage, za naše književne prilike pojave u svakome pogledu markantne. Riječi su mu po smislu često mutne i zbunjene, nejasne i potpuno zamagljene, ali se između stihova osjeća podzemni huk nevidljive tamne ponornice, što se tu valja pod tim riječima istinito i sudbonosno.

Part II

TRANSLATIONS

For notes on the literal nature of these translations, and on the occasional use of the present tense in narrative passages, see pages ix and 167.

1 *Terror in a Railway-train*

DRAGUTIN TADIJANOVIĆ

In my tenth year, in May 1915, for the first time I travelled by railway, from Brod to Vrpolje. My mother and grandmother took me; we were going on a visit to my father, to Đakovo. At that time, for a few months he was the batman of a military doctor who was called, if I remember rightly, Tallian, from Osijek. They took a basket of strawberries with them, too, as a present for that doctor.

It is as if there is even now in my bones the terror that I suffered until the guard had examined the travel tickets. Before his arrival my mother had said to me:

'Draw yourself in. Draw yourself in, so that you're not so big.'

'How shall I draw myself in? I don't know that,' I answered crossly.

Grandmother added:

'Obey your mother. Is it really difficult for you to draw yourself in?'

I was, in fact, rather well developed for my age; they were afraid that they would have to pay for a full ticket for me too, and not a half, as for children under ten. And I had a half ticket, which I was holding carefully in my hand.

When the guard entered the compartment the first whom he noticed was me. I began to tremble from fear. He said to me:

'Get up, little boy. Let me see how big you are.'

Trying to draw in my shoulders as much as possible I rose, huddled up, and went up to my mother, terrified.

'Is that your son?' he asked mother.

Grandmother answered, more quickly:

'Yes, sir. And he is my grandson.'

'Has he a ticket?'

'Of course he has.'

'Let me see.'

And I timidly handed the guard my half ticket. But he said to my mother and grandmother:

'Do you two think that I don't see? He's older than ten.'

'But he's not, sir, he's not!' they exclaimed in one voice.

'How—he's not? You see how big he is. Don't you tell me. I've a good eye.'

I trembled like a reed in water. Mother answered once more:

'He is not, sir, he's not. He'll be ten about All Saints' Day. That's when he was born.'

'I see well, and too well.'

The guard again turned his glance on me; I was dying of fright, only I didn't burst into tears.

'Give your tickets,' he ordered sternly. And he quickly punched them.

He came up to me and with his hand shook my shoulder a little.

'Don't be afraid, brave chap! All right, all right, carry on.'

He turned to the other travellers, and grandmother began to console me and give me courage, for him to hear too.

'The gentleman won't do anything to you. You see he's kind.'

From my eyes tears dropped—because of his kindness.

2 From a narrative *We Three*

DRAGUTIN TADIJANOVIĆ

Not expecting that anyone would come near to where I was, I sat down on a mound near the head of Vojnović's grave, beside a cypress; I drew out my notebook and crossing my legs I wrote the first five lines. The basic thought that I planned to express in the poem was not completely clear to me. I was lifting my head over the paper, glancing around.

Suddenly that boy appeared before me.

I had not in the least expected him.

I close my notebook, and between the two of us a conversation begins again.

'Do you know who is lying in this grave?'

'They told me—some poet.'

'What is he called?'

'I don't know.'

'Read his name. You know how to read, yourself.'

'*Here rests the poet Ivo Vojnović, 1857–1929.*'

'If you attend schools and go in for studies you will hear a lot about him.'

'Look! On that grave there's a picture of a boy!'

'I know, I've seen it.'

My little interlocutor went up to a neighbouring grave beside a wall, and gazed, from close to, at the picture of the dead boy. Slowly he began to read the words engraved beneath the picture: *Do not forget us, Milo.*

He said, still more loudly:

'Milo was the name of my aunt's son.'

'Did you know him?'

'No.'

'What is his surname?'

'Stanković.'

'On that grave is written: Stanković.'

'Oh yes. Then that's my aunt's son, Milo. He was killed.'

'Killed? When?'

'In the war. During the bombing. He was going along, he was holding his hands on the top of his head, and an aeroplane threw a bomb, and the shrapnel hit him on the head, and everything was bloody, his hands too. He was twelve years old.'

'Didn't you know that he is buried here?'

'No. Now I see. So that is Milo.'

Again he went up to the boy's picture and began to contemplate it attentively.

'He has a white cap on his head.'

'Yes,' I said aloud, but I thought: 'As if he sensed that death had chosen, for itself, precisely that place on his body to lay him level with the ground.'

We two did not utter a single word more.

3 From a narrative *Šimo Šimić*

DRAGUTIN TADIJANOVIĆ

I will talk, as I have promised, about Šimo Šimić.

One Saturday—it was in December 1917—my grandfather returned late at night, with the cart, from Sijekovac.

Grandmother and my mother were waiting up for him, as always.

But grandfather was not alone. With him was a boy of some fifteen years, in torn clothes, with rags on his feet, bare-headed, thin, frozen. He was coughing—no, he was racked with coughing.

'And who's that?' asked grandmother.

'He'll mind the cows for us. You know yourself that we haven't a cowherd.'

While grandmother and mother were unharnessing the horses, the two of them—grandfather and the unknown boy—came into the warm room. When grandfather had turned up the wick of the oil lamp it shone more powerfully, and from my bed I glanced at the boy, who was trembling from cold as if seven fevers shook him. He was a few years older than I, taller than I, but it seemed to me then that he was not more than eleven or twelve, and I thought: 'This is the poverty, misery, about which I've only heard until now.' I caught that quick glance of his, a little scared, with which he was observing the room and me; he halted it finally on the big home-made loaf, on the table prepared for grandfather's supper.

I did not take my eyes off that boy as long as the two of them, he and grandfather, were having supper, and grandfather was urging him:

'Take some, take more!'

I was thinking: 'Where will he sleep?'

When supper was finished, grandfather calls him:

'Now you come along with me. I'll show you where you'll spend the night.'

And they went out. I thought: 'If I were in his place, how terrified I'd be!'

For a long, long time I couldn't get to sleep.

He was sleeping in the hayloft. In the hay. In pitch darkness.

In the morning, when I awoke, he was already in the room, dressed in warmer clothes, shod in leather peasant's shoes, bright red in the face.

He was looking through the window, to the village. He didn't want to see me.

We were both silent.

I should have liked him to ask me something. But he behaved as though I didn't exist.

There was heard only the ticking of the clock with long slender chains, on the wall beside the other window, that one where, at night, grandmother slept.

I broke the silence, exited, and asked him almost in a whisper: 'Listen to me! What are you called?'

'What does it matter to you?' he answered more loudly, not turning round.

'I'm asking you. I'd like to know what your name is.'

'Šimo.'

'And what else? Surname!'

'Šimić.'

'Where do you come from?'

'I won't tell you!' He suddenly turns and looks at me.

If I'm not mistaken, his eyes were full of tears. I said to him: 'And you needn't, Šimo. I shall know it from my granddad.'

'Well, know it then!'

Again there was silence until my mother came into the room and called me:

'Get up, it's late already. The sun came out long ago.'

And so, what am I to relate—how it was from one day to another, the whole winter, until spring?

I went on foot to Brod, to school, and Šimo minded the cows. From grandfather he got a sheepskin-lined coat and a leather bag with a strap over the shoulder, which grandmother would fill for him with bread, bacon, cheese, onion, something of that sort each day.

As soon as the snow thawed he drove the cows to Dolovi, to Pribudovac, and towards evening he returned home with them. Nobody ever heard him start singing, like the other cowherds. He would finish the evening jobs, in the shed, in the yard, and then have supper, and then he would climb into the hayloft and fall asleep.

But would he perhaps not fall asleep, but gaze long into the darkness with open eyes?

He would not tell anyone whether he had a father, a mother, a brother, a sister. Where they were. How they lived.

My grandfather had found him in Sijekovac, alone, frozen through, hungry; he had driven him home, fed him, clothed him, and now he, Šimo Šimić, is pondering, pondering long, how he could manage to get to his own home, somewhere far away, across the Sava, there where he had been born and had grown up among his own people.

Spring came; primroses pushed through the grass.

Šimo Šimić for the first time went off with the cows to Sječe, to the Marić hill, from where he saw the Sava and Brod, through which that night he had driven with my grandfather; he spied, in the distance, his Bosnia.

Whose voice did he hear, that was calling him to come?

When deep night had already fallen the cows still did not return.

'Hasn't he perhaps run away?' someone from my family said.

Yes. He never more returned to us.

I've long remembered him, Šimo Šimić. Well, as you see, even today.

4 A folk tale *The Lion and the Man*

from a collection by TVRTKO ČUBELIĆ

An old lioness had reared a young lion in the midst of a desert, and instilled into his breast hatred towards man, who had killed his father and two brothers.

When the young lion had grown up and felt that his strength was great he took leave of his mother, promising that he would not for so long have any peace until he found and destroyed his greatest enemy—man.

He travelled a long time, ceaselessly seeking what he had set out after. On the expanse of a sea of sand he once encountered a large animal with a long curved neck, covered with dark brown hair, with two humps on his back. Immediately he asked it angrily:

'You're a man, aren't you?'

The camel sighed and calmly answered him:

'No. A man looks different. You consider that I am a powerful creature. I am; nobody can endure hunger and thirst as long as I can. Nobody can catch me up when I speed over this sandy waste. And yet I am man's slave. I kneel before him when he wishes to mount me; he directs all my strength to his own use, and for this permits me to feed myself with prickly plants. Then after my death man strips off my skin to make a tent from it for himself, to shelter himself from the hot sun and bad weather. No, I am not a man.'

The young lion pondered, and went on further. Now he came upon a strange animal. On its forehead it had two horns. Its neck was thick and strong. When the lion approached it it struck powerfully with its foot against the ground. 'This will be a man,' thought the lion, and immediately asked:

'Are you a man?'

'I, a man? You're wildly mistaken, my dear fellow. I am his servant, and he is the master over us all. He fixes a yoke on to my neck, and I must plough and draw the greatest burdens. He eats my flesh and makes shoes for himself from my skin.'

The lion frowned, and went on further.

Going thus, he caught the sound of some trampling: the earth seemed to shake, and see, a tall noble animal came running up. The long mane on its neck sprang away and its long tail waved behind.

'Ha! you are a man!' said the lion.

The horse, neighing, stopped and sadly answered:

'I am not. I am man's servant.'

'Are you really his servant? But see how strong and proud you are!'

'So I am when I am alone. But when I am near a man then my pride wilts. He thrusts a bit into my mouth, bridles me, and mounts me, and I must carry him wherever he likes. Power is man's, and we are all nothing in comparison with him.'

Now the lion stole away into a forest. He heard some blows, as if someone was chopping wood. He drew near to see what it was. There he saw some smallish creature, insignificant in comparison with himself. He had just felled a gigantic fir tree; there remained only the lower part of the trunk, the stump, two spans high above the ground. The lion asked this stranger whether he had seen a man anywhere.

'You're looking for a man?' answered the man. 'What would you want with him?'

'He killed my father and two brothers; I want to take revenge on him.'

'Well, that's good, really good. May Allah help you!'

This praise pleased the lion. He related all that he had heard about his father and his brothers. He also begged the man just to continue his work.

The man had just hacked into the tree stump, so he asked

the lion to help him. The lion asked how he would help him.

'I haven't a wedge to put into this cleft. Be so kind as to thrust your foot inside.'

'I will, with pleasure.'

As soon as the lion thrust his foot into the cleft the man drew out the hatchet and the lion's foot was clutched in the crack. The lion was caught.

Only then did the man tell him that he was a man.

'I see what it is,' the lion sighed. 'If it were a matter of strength you would not be so terrible, but your skill does that. And now you will kill me, won't you?'

'No, I won't. I'll let you go, so that you may go and tell how man's skill is more powerful than the greatest force. But he sometimes has a merciful heart, too. For otherwise he would not be—man.'

5   From an article *And Trebnje was Born*

from the magazine *Review*

Trebnje, a little Slovene village halfway between Zagreb and Ljubljana, with barely a hundred houses, situated in the poorest commune of Slovenia, has become an important meeting place of Yugoslav primitive painters. The first meeting represented ten exciting days for these painters, who hitherto were unacquainted with each other, and perhaps had not even heard of each other. The whole population took part. Each day the local people came to watch their guests working on glass, linen and wood. At the end the works were placed along a wall, because there were no suitable premises for an exhibition.

The artists, in return for hospitality and travel expenses, had to paint one painting each and leave it to Trebnje. From the paintings which they left a permanent gallery has been formed. Now Trebnje, in addition to a yearly salon which the most important Yugoslav personalities open, has a well-arranged permanent gallery and four independent exhibitions annually, two from Slovenia and two from other republics.

6 From an article *Mountain Tourism*

from the magazine *Review*

Mostly the shores of the warm Adriatic sea attract the tourists. The great indentation of the Yugoslav sea coast has formed a whole succession of bays, larger or smaller, with peninsulas and promontories, with islands and inlets, quiet little coves and sandy beaches. Along the whole coast, whose length amounts to over 2,000 kilometres, are ranged more than a thousand smaller or bigger islands. Therefore they have called Yugoslavia 'The land with a thousand islands.'

But as well as the sea Yugoslavia has also lovely mountain regions. From the Alpine mountains in the extreme north-west to the picturesque lakes and river valleys in the Macedonian south, the interior is also full of varied landscapes. However, the inaccessibility of some of the most beautiful districts in Yugoslavia and the shortage of hotels in these regions have caused them to remain unrevealed for tourists. Only in recent years, with the construction of more and more modern motor roads and means of communication, and by the erection of hotels, are the doors being slowly opened in the mountainous expanses.

7 From an article *Hell in a Valley of Paradise*

from the magazine *Review*

The valley of the River Soča, in Slovenia, is one of the loveliest in Yugoslavia. To travel up the Soča represents an experience which is not easily forgotten.

Not far from Tolmin, a pretty little town in the Soča valley, high up in the mountains, where only the foot of the experienced mountaineer can tread, nestles the hamlet Čadrg.

A legend relates that during the time of his exile from Florence the great Italian poet Dante stopped for a considerable time in Čadrg, Tolmin and their neighbourhood. This region impressed him so much that he came every day to a charmingly situated cave above a stream, the Zalaščica, which winds through the hundred-metre-deep chasm, down below, of a magnificent ravine. Dante—as the legend says—would sit on a rock in front of the cave in his scarlet cloak, with a cap of the same colour on his head. He was always writing something, and in the early evening he would descend by winding goats' and wolves' paths through the rocky wilderness towards Tolmin. The legend even relates that Dante, inspired by the unique landscapes and the savage beauty of the fearsome canyon, wrote his most magnificent work, *The Divine Comedy*.

8 From an article *The Grey-haired Poet's Long Journey*

from the magazine *Review*

One cold winter's night in 1942 the 66-year-old poet Vladimir Nazor, together with his young friend the poet Ivan Goran Kovačić, the author of the moving poem *The Pit*, started out for, and finally reached, the National-Liberation Army.

The poet spoke here, too, from the front. He was a source of encouragement to the men in a hard time of suffering. They loved him and looked after him. And the Commander-in-Chief, Marshal Tito, issued precise instructions that the life of the Partisans should be alleviated, as far as possible, for the aged poet.

· · · · ·

After the breach of the encirclement in the very powerful fifth offensive, at the time when the Partisan units, hungry and exhausted, were surrounded by the enemy, many times superior in strength, the Supreme Command was located on a hill near a Bosnian village from which the inhabitants had fled into the forest, in terror of cruel retaliation by the Germans. Vladimir Nazor was so exhausted that they carried him. But even then, and in many other difficult times, he was ready for a joke.

Nearby, in a hut, was Vladimir Zečević, who had been a priest before he took up arms. The Partisans called him Father Vlado.

Having heard that among the Partisans there was a priest, some old women picked a basket of strawberries and went off to the priest for him to forgive them their sins and bless them, for one might be killed at any moment. Instead of Father Vlado the old women came upon Vlado Nazor, who likewise had a beard.

'Father, bless us!' And the old women assumed a pious pose.

'Be blessed,' exclaimed the poet readily, 'as far as I'm concerned. Leave the strawberries here. Ask for a proper blessing there, in that hut.' And he pointed to where the refuge of Father Vlado Zečević was.

9 Extracts from the short story *Evening*

ANTONIJE ISAKOVIĆ

I knew that supper would not be ready for two hours yet, so I decided to spend that time sitting on the stone slab.

I was tired, I felt a certain pressure inside me, like a famished man. I was not hungry, for as soon as I had arrived they had offered me American cheese. I had cut that yellow canned cheese with a knife, and thought how the war had become easier for me. And now I thought this again, seeing a girl comrade shaking out rugs in front of the headquarters. I should sleep on a rug which I was not going to carry!

I reached for a pebble, and tossed it in front of me.

Before me stood two young girls. Only then did I see them. Both were of the same height, only one was plumper and had dark pigtails, tossed forward. The other timid and more slender; I did not see her hair, it was hidden beneath a white kerchief.

No doubt they had been observing me for a long time. The plumper one said:

'Comrade, can we tell each other things?'

The question surprised me: she didn't say 'talk' but 'tell'. What have we to tell? Clumsily I turned my tobacco case over in my hand.

'Yes, we can,' I said.

They came lightly up and sat down beside me, one on one side, the other on the other. It seemed to me that both were breathing deeply, as if they had been running.

I now noticed that the slimmer one was not so dark as the plumper one. That she had beautiful dark eyes and a long curve of the eyebrows. But the plumper one had developed from the physique of a wild young mountain maid. Both were in white shirts of hemp, only the slimmer one had a short black tunic on.

'You are sisters?'

'Yes, but not born ones. By our uncles.'

'These are our houses.' The slimmer girl indicated them with her hand.

I was silent and waited for them to ask me something. From beneath the stone slab a cricket chirped. Far down below the dark rye stirred. In that wide field of rye large white heaps stood out—stones thrown down.

'Those are piles of stones?' I asked.

'We're clearing the meadows; our land is like that. You see that biggest pile? This year I've cleared that part,' said the plumper girl.

'Like graves,' I said.

'Yes, graves.' The girl sighed deeply.

I feared lest I had reminded them of men who were killed. This was free territory and all able males were with the Partisans. Suddenly I asked:

'You're called Gora?'

'No, but I *am* like a mountain'—she jerked her shoulders. 'Call me that.'

'And you?'

The slimmer girl glanced at me timidly, and I was surprised by her answer:

'Invent one for me, too.'

I said the first that occurred to me:

'Slim-figure.'

'It's very long.'

'Well then, I'll call you Cathode. Do you like that?'

'It sounds strange. What is it?'

'It's something slender, nice.'

'But you gave me a peasant's name: Gora!'

'Well—now I wouldn't be able to think up anything else. We can talk without names,' I said quickly.

Suddenly Gora asked me:

'And the war, when will it end?'

'We shall win!'

'I know that, but when will it end?' She repeated the question almost as if offended.

'I don't know.' And I raised my shoulders.

'You don't know? Well then, who must know?'

'Well . . .'

'This autumn.' The girl seized me by the hand.

'But it's autumn now!'

'But it's only just begun.' And the slimmer girl seized me by the hand.

'Yes, begun'—Gora caught on.

'But autumn is short in your parts.'

'Well, all right, will it end this winter?'

'I don't know.'

'Say this winter. What kind of man are you? Winter is long in our part. We're using up the whole forest as fuel—how can it not be over?' Both girls looked at me with terror.

'If not this winter, then next year at this time it will be all over with the war.'

'That's a very long time,' said Gora, and clasped her side.

'It's not, it will pass quickly. And whom do you have in the war?'

Again I was surprised at the answer.

'Nobody!' they both replied together.

'How's that?'

'We haven't any brothers. And when the young men went off we still weren't grown girls,' said Gora.

'Now you are.'

'A long time already.'

For some time we were silent and my hands were in theirs. Beneath us the cricket chirped.

'And you, where are you from?' The first question that the more slender girl had directed to me.

'That's not important. You can see that he's one of ours.'

'I want to know.' And that obstinacy of hers delighted me.

'From Serbia,' I answered.

'A Serb,' said the girl, drawing it out. 'I thought that they were tall.'

'There are various kinds of us.'

'And before the war didn't you ever come to our parts?'

'No.'

'Our people used to come to you.'

'Well, Serbia is a rich country,' said Gora seriously. 'What is there in our part? "Šipad". And there haven't always been jobs for our people.'

'And before, did you know about our districts?'

'I learned in school.'

'About Glamočko Plain?'

'Yes, about Glamočko Plain.'

'It's nice to study at school,' the slimmer girl said sincerely. 'And did you imagine that everything in our part was like this?'

'No, I didn't.'

'And what didn't you?'

'The mountains—they're very high.'

'Our teacher had a big map, and I saw Serbia on it.'

'But these war ones of yours are very detailed,' said Gora. 'Everything is in them, even our houses. Only there isn't this one, where the headquarters are placed. We built it last year.'

'Built? Strange!'

'There were some beams cut,' said Gora.

'We dragged the building material from "Šipad",' said the girl in the black tunic. 'Father says: "They can drag away beams but they can't a building." '

I burst into laughter.

In the headquarters an acetylene lamp was burning. Around its large flame a butterfly flew.

I observed Gora's hand, and saw on her middle finger a simple ring.

'A ring?' I said.

She nodded.

'You were given it?'

'No, our young men are at the war.'

'I have one, too,' said the girl in the black tunic.

'We gave them to each other,' Gora said drily. 'A ring means the same in your part?'

'Yes: love,' I answered quickly.

'We don't know that.' And both stared down into the dark rye field.

I felt their hot palms beginning to clasp me tightly. I too began slowly to move my hands. Their fingers caressed my hand. Inside my shirt I felt sweat around my spine. Immediately the idea came to me—why doesn't one of them go away? There they sat on, and looked down into the rye, which rustled like silk.

'There's no moon,' I said suddenly.

'It's better like this,' said Gora.

'It comes out only about midnight,' said the girl in the tunic.

'Aren't you going?' Gora asked me.

'Where to?'

'There,' and she pointed with her head towards the headquarters.

'No, I shan't.'

'Are you going on guard tonight?'

'No, I'm not.'

.   .   .   .   .

Someone lit a battery lamp in front of the headquarters. One moment it gave out a green, red, then a white eye of light. It was illuminating some chest.

I smoke a cigarette and think how to free myself from one of them. It seemed to me that I wanted both equally. I freed my hands and felt them seize at them at the same moment. The girl in the black tunic caressed more tenderly, and Gora more hungrily, more feverishly.

'I'd like to drink some water,' I said.

I held my breath, so that I might know, by my hand, which would go. They both looked at my boots; in the brief silence all three hearts were heard clearly. I repeated, with trepidation:

'I'm thirsty.'

They both suddenly stood up.

'We'll bring some right away'—I don't know who said it.

When I was left alone, desperate, I stretched out my legs and lit a fresh cigarette. I stretched myself out across the whole step, something tickled me about the neck and I longed to bathe in cold water.

The girls were coming, and I drew in my legs. Gora was carrying a drinking vessel and the other an earthenware utensil.

'We've no sugar.'

'That doesn't matter. I'm thirsty.'

They both sat down again and the girl in the black tunic put the earthenware vessel down beside her.

I observed them furtively, to discover whether they hadn't discussed something between them. I drew back a little and looked at their rigid faces.

They were observing each other, they hated each other now, and I did not dare to look at them openly. Gora's half-open lips moved slightly. I sensed that she was saying to her sister: 'Run away, why do you sit there? I'm the elder, you forget that! I saw him first and he's mine.' Gora was bending her head a little, and in her eyes had collected little shiny beads.

The girl in the black tunic was looking at her wonderingly. It was as though she were saying: 'Why are you angry with me? You see, he liked speaking with me, too. With me he talked more seriously, and he gave me the nicest name, which I've forgotten. Do you think that he's caressing only your hand? You want to say that you are the elder? There isn't an elder one here.'

I bit my lip and thought: 'Come on, let one of you two go away. The left one or the right one, it's all the same. Perhaps I ought to say. Say to which one? Or get up and go?'

.   .   .   .   .

The door of their house opened and the hearth threw light on us. Our clumsy shadows flickered about the uneven yard. I saw in the centre my own, the tallest, and two wheels at the side. Three soldiers were to be seen in front of the headquarters. Someone was calling my name, long drawn out.

'They're calling someone,' said Gora.

'Yes, they're calling,' I repeated absently.

'You?'

'Yes, me.'

'To supper.'

'Probably,' I said wearily.

Again was heard the long-drawn-out voice, and a soldier was explaining that he had seen me up above, underneath the pine trees.

Soon the clink of spoons and the smell of boiled potato began to reach us. I wanted them to stop eating as soon as possible. Someone praised the cook loudly. Beneath us the cricket again began to chirp, the stone slab was still warm. Gora pulled me by the arm, bent towards me, and I noticed dark fists in her shirt. She looks straight at me, I feel she wants to say something to me. She is repressing the words within herself, her throat moves dumbly. She raises her arm, and the wide sleeve drops downwards.

'You see that pile of mine. Tomorrow evening I'll be there.'

Both sisters suddenly rose and went indoors.

I remained alone and looked at the dark rye field, at Gora's big white pile of stones. And I heard music. A soldier had kept some promise of his. It was playing loudly, it was a military march.

I had stretched out my legs and was lying on the wide step. Someone called:

'Hi, where's the news?'

The soldier said in self-defence that he had found the wavelength.

'Change it!' shouted the same voice.

Then there came the sound of a piano, and it wandered around the wooden houses.

'Change it!' shouted the voice, but I wished that the piano might be left on as long as possible.

I lay there; behind me the pine trees were stirring; the cricket became silent, and the stone was still warm.

No doubt I slept a long time. The moon was burning in the rye field. I stood up and went quickly towards the largest heap of stones. By the heap I caught sight of Gora's back and the thick pitch-black plait tossed across to her hips. The moon was ringing out above the field, we were standing one beside the other, when out of the tall rye emerged the girl in the black tunic.

Again we were all three sitting and looking at the gleaming rye.

From a monologue *My Son*

IVAN SLAMNIG

There are many ways in which my son could be living. Indeed, when I think about those ways I see that I have a great deal to think about.

My son could be somewhere in South America. He may be in one of those lovely capitals which are called Lima, Bogotá, Caracas. Or Rio de Janeiro. In that case he is dressed in a white suit, a soft white suit; in it he goes out in the evening on to a terrace—when I imagine Rio de Janeiro it's always evening, and men go out on to spacious terraces in white suits, the wind blows lightly from the ocean or La Plata or something like that, and men in light white smoking-jackets drink iced drinks. Pieces of ice float in the green like huge jewels.

He undoubtedly has money. He earns it, with his ability. He has a canned beef factory, and he is enormously rich. And now, on the terrace among all those beautiful women, each of whom would like to have him, he is conducting business matters, business conversations. He laughs his harsh southerner's laugh. He looks like a real South American. Together with this he is firm, businesslike. It's no joke to acquire, in such a short time, such a large factory. Look at these serpents' eyes of the dazzling women around him. Take care, son!

Perhaps he has some girl friend. I believe that he has known how to choose well, although I should have liked to have taken part in it, I too. Actually, I don't know whether I should have liked to. Let him choose her himself. He has chosen her himself. She is a foreigner. I don't understand what she says, and we shall feel a little strange towards each other, but I know that this is only temporary and perhaps only appears so, for whoever my son loves I too must love. Yes, he is finding me a daughter-in-law, beautiful, rich.

There are other rumours, too, there are other possibilities. It's quite a job to imagine all this together, but it's interesting. Actually it doesn't worry me whether it's a job nor whether it's interesting. I sit and think about it. I must think, for I must find a solution which satisfies everything. If we analyse the situation in South America, I mean his situation in South America, we see that there's a good deal which won't quite do, and we would find in that possibility a fair number of flaws. I must consider that case still more carefully.

He might be in some other place. He might be, let's say, somewhere in the north, let's say in Norway. When I think about that better it seems to me that he is somewhere far away in the north, he's walking in high boots and a sailor's leather storm helmet. What is he walking about in? I think that he's walking about in a pile of fish. He's the owner of a fishing boat, he takes part in great fishing expeditions for herring and cod and similar fish in which those northern seas abound. I don't know what to think about this—that he has gone on a hunt for whales. Yes, it could be that. He has gone on a whale-hunting expedition, somewhere, among icy mountains. He's shouting, and his voice echoes from one icy hill to another. He has been at sea a long long time already, he's expecting some special catch, he has some reasons of his own. He's not even in Norway, he's somewhere around the South Pole. Whales are hunted there now, particularly, they've told me. He's far away amid the ice, he's carrying out some enterprise, I know that it's a question of something big, of some great gain and glory. Of course he has had misfortunes too, he has been lost in a desert of ice, he passed the winter once or twice among ice floes; such things do occur, we have all heard about that already. This possibility has the advantage that an explanation can be found for the fact that he doesn't write.

For that is rather an important question. That must be kept in sight.

(*Perhaps the rain, somewhere in Bosnia, is deluging his grave.*)

He may even be quite near, comparatively. Perhaps he's in Italy. Perhaps even in Trieste. I don't know how he has come by money. I think—I say 'think' on account of you people, because I am really convinced—that at the beginning he was engaged a little in black-marketeering. He was dealing on the black market in cigarettes. It can't be considered that it is anything wicked to deal in cigarettes on the black market. They are a luxury, and anyone who is ready to pay a high price for that, let him pay for it. If he is indeed dealing on the black market let him be dealing in cigarettes. I would understand him and forgive if he had been dealing even in something else, but still it pleases me most that he's dealt in cigarettes. He's good at finding his way about, thank God; I think that he inherited this from my side. One of my brothers is very similar to him in that. He had to find some way to come by money, enough money to be able to pass on to bigger undertakings which would be more profitable and more honest. I have not yet decided whether in Trieste he has a big textile firm or a big provision firm. Whatever it is, they are large, beautiful premises illuminated with fluorescent strip lighting; everything gives an impression of such freshness, the tinned fruits and salami sausages look colourful and gleam in the shop windows. Only the better-class people come into his stores. He himself is not so often in there. People know, really, when the boss comes into the shop. The old customers who like him to serve them himself know. He is there, the expert, quick and obliging but yet dignified. There is one woman who always comes at the times when he is in the shop. She orders various trifles, always some foolish things. The fact is that she comes because of him, obviously. They exchange glances while he is wrapping up fifteen decagrams of ham. Their hands touch. She would like to have him. I think that she attracts him, too. As for me, I should like to know something in more detail about that girl. Today one cannot have confidence in anybody, and Trieste is a big city, there are all sorts in it. I don't know whether she loves his white teeth and black hair or his shop with such great piles of expensive materials.

The last one who saw him was some man named Nedžad. The last as far as I know, that is to say. From Nedžad originates the last reliable piece of news that I know about him. This is what Nedžad relates:

'Both of us were in the National Guard, and we were thinking of transferring to the Partisans. We were in the National Guard, and we had contact with the Partisans. We used to cross from one side to the other. We two were a sort of between-army.

'For a long time there hadn't been any very great concentration in that area. Then suddenly that area became important, Germans, Circassians, Četniks, Ustaše and every devil came there; I don't know what they were up to. And so we went along a road. So we came to a big lime tree, where the road divided. And then he said: "I'll go to the left, and off you go, to the right. When we pass this thicket we shall meet again." And so he went left and I right. And then I didn't dare to go out of the thicket, but I stayed there the whole afternoon and spent the night there, and the next day in the morning there wasn't a trace of anybody, not even of him, and I hid in my village, in a hayloft, until the end of the war.'

Nedžad has said that much. Nobody had witnessed anything else. How many black coffees Nedžad has drunk at my home! And yet I haven't found out where they were going, nor what he was scared of in the thicket.

It is clear that he went somewhere. He didn't stay there. First of all comes the question—which way, and how, did he go somewhere?

It is most probable that he fled to the Partisans. I have made enquiries as to which Partisan unit was at that time in that area. I have talked with men who could have been from that unit. They confirmed that in that area there were cases of men transferring. Of course I've made enquiries in particular about my son. I've described him, and they told me it may have been that someone did transfer who would answer to that description. Lots of them transferred.

I also learned, further, that some wounded men from that unit were taken across to Bari. It's easily possible that they took him too across to Bari. It's quite possible that he too was wounded.

(*Perhaps the rain, somewhere in Bosnia, is deluging his grave.*)

11 From the novel *Give us this Day*

RADOMIR KONSTANTINOVIĆ

I'd like to dance, she said. My whole life I've been dreaming
that I'm dancing. I wanted to go to the sea, and to dance on
some hotel terrace above the sea. At the wedding I didn't
dance either. And now I'd like to get up out of bed and go off to
dance. We were sitting at a big table. Do you want us to dance?
I asked him. No, he said. He told me that he did not like
dancing and that he was tired. He was pale, and looked at me
continually. He was holding me by the hand. He pressed me
with his hand, under the table. He trod on me. I had white
shoes. And I was all in white, she said. I was afraid lest he soil
my shoes. There were many people around us. They had all
come. They were laughing and shouting. He was pleased. I
want it to be known, he said, how it is when Edward Kraus
gets married. Then he bent over me. Are you sorry, he
asked me, that we didn't drive in a cab? I said I wasn't sorry.
(These violins, these violins.) I said I wanted to dance. He said
he had wanted us to go on foot because he wished that everyone
might see what kind of wife Edward Kraus had got. Let them
see, he murmured in my ear. I want to dance, I said. He trod on
me with his foot. It hurts, I said, and I want to dance. He said
that he was tired. And you can't dance with anyone else, he said.
Today you are with me. Today it's different. Quite different.
Quite different from other times, he told me. He was sweating.
Why are you sweating so? I asked him. He shook his head.
I don't know, he said to me. This happens once in a lifetime,
only once, he affirmed. I burst into laughter. Oh, I said, are
you really sure? He hung his head. I'd kill you, he said, if you
should once more experience this with someone else. I laughed.
I was angry because he wouldn't dance with me. The others

were dancing. I wanted to dance like the others. I didn't want
us to sit at the table, to hold each other by the hand and watch
others dancing. I laughed. No, I said, I was thinking that we
should get married again. It's so lovely now, I told him. It's so
lovely, I said. I'll stand up, I suddenly told him, and I'll dance
alone if you won't. I was laughing. Around us they were dancing. He was pale. No, no, he begged, you mustn't do that, he
begged me. I laughed. Alone, alone, I said. You'll see. Then he
looked at me with dull eyes. I thought that he was drunk. I don't
know how to dance, he said. My whole life, he said, I've been
waiting for this day. And I haven't danced, he said. I thought
that it was fine that I hadn't danced in all my life. Don't you
think that's fine? Do you think that every man can pride himself on this? he asked me. No, I said, and I stopped laughing.
Not every man can pride himself on this. Around us they were
still dancing. They were playing trumpets and violins, and
beating drums. I listened and watched, but suddenly it wasn't
the same as before. Edward and I were sitting at that big table.
On the table plates were left, and wine glasses, dishes, trays.
Some flowers. Breadcrumbs, remains of food. Cigarettes, put
out. One cigarette was smoking. Put it out, I said to Edward. He
didn't seem to hear me. He was staring in front of him. I knew
that he could not see those who were dancing. They were only
dancing. One man was lying at the end of the table. He was
asleep. Wine had been spilled around his head. Suddenly it
seemed to me that they had all abandoned us, that they were all
like enemies to us, and that Edward and I were condemned to
loneliness for ever. Between us and the others there was a great
silence, a kind of indifference. Perhaps some cold air. Just like
that. Then, there, beyond that silence, that cold air, that indifference, the music was playing. We were alone. They were
dancing. We were frightened, and held each other by the hand.
Alone. Put out that cigarette, I said to Edward again, and
suddenly I began to cry. The people will go, I thought. And
I didn't know whether it was better that they go at once and

never return there any more, to those rooms, and dance, and that the music play, or better that they stay a little longer. Perhaps I feared both. Perhaps I was afraid to remain alone with Edward by that table with the remains of food. Everything reminded me of them, of those people, of those who had been together. I cried. Edward gripped me still more firmly by the hands. I will learn to dance, he said, don't cry. I'll buy a gramophone, he said, you'll see. And then you will teach me to dance. That will be funny, he said, it will be very funny and you will laugh. I'll dance and you'll laugh. I so lanky, he whispered in my ear, and so funny. But I have never danced, I wanted to live for this day. But you are crying, he whispered, as if I can't buy a gramophone, and as if you won't teach me to dance. Anna—he called me as if I were far away from him (but I was sitting beside him and we were alone at that big table)—Anna, promise me that you will teach me to dance. Promise me. I'm terribly fond of dancing, he said. Promise me.

Suddenly she became silent. She was looking at me, but I knew that she did not see me. She was seeing the wedding, herself and Edward sitting at a large table. She was seeing the others dancing. Edward was vowing that he would buy a gramophone. He was whispering in her ear how happy he would be when he danced. (Oh, she would laugh a lot then.) That was how he was thinking. But that wasn't the whole story. No, I remembered, that wasn't the whole story. She felt that they were alone. Suddenly that they were left alone, for ever. Do you want to see? she asked me. I nodded my head. She went to the cupboard. She opened it and turned things over a bit in it. Then she returned with a large packet of photographs. She undid the blue ribbon which bound the packet. The photographs spread about the table. She was selecting from among them, searching. And then she found the photograph from the wedding. The steps of the Cathedral. Sunshine. They were standing on those steps. Anna and Edward in the centre.

She was in a long white dress, with flowers in her arms. She was laughing. She looked happy. But no, I said to myself, she was not happy. If she had been, I said, she would not need to suffer now. She would be lying peacefully on the bed. The gramophone record revolved. Violins and drums. A piano. Her eyes were dull. The photographer, invisible, was waving his long thin arms. He was bending, across his head fell the large black cloth. He was peering into the glass of his old-fashioned wooden photographic apparatus on a trestle. He, the un-acknowledged artist. He who must have sensed the secret of time, who tried to halt people, in time, in happiness and un-happiness, he who fought against that time. Old photo-grapher, I whispered, you who fought against time. What has become of that time, and where have the traces of it disappeared to? A man must be happy for once. Once he must die. But, I trembled, what death am I speaking of? There is no such death. Once again she is there where Edward Kraus is. It is there where Anna is. And it will come to her, I said. It will come some day. Look. She was holding flowers in her arms. Over her was standing a man. He was laughing. The others were holding each other by the hand. Anna was waiting, her attention strained. The flowers could drop from her arms at any moment. To scatter.

But I didn't teach him to dance, she said. And we never danced. Afterwards it was all too late, she whispered. She threw down the photograph. I knew that. I knew that it was too late. We could have danced. We could have not danced, too, she said. It was too late. One day he came from the town carrying something. Anna, he said, I have brought a gramo-phone. But it was too late. I knew that. A gramophone? I asked him. Why have you brought a gramophone? He looked at me, exultant. Poor Edward. Have you really forgotten? he asked me. He wanted us to dance. Perhaps he too had heard some sea. Perhaps he too understood that happiness must be finished with. But I don't think so. No, I said to him, we can't dance now. I went away into the corridor. I was crying. With one hand I was supporting myself against the wall, and I was crying. Behind me the door opened. He was at it. I turned. I looked at him. He was tall, in the light of the doorway. Outside the town was hooting. The town was talking. He was terribly tall. Don't you want us to dance? he whispered. Come back, for us to dance, he said to me. No, I said, no, no, Edward, I told him, how can you not understand that? No, I told him.

She sighed. I rejected him, she said.

12 From the short story *The Miracle at Olovo*

IVO ANDRIĆ

Day was dawning when they emerged on to the first heights
above Sarajevo. The little girl, who until then had complained
a good deal, protested, and cried, was now resting in a specially
adapted shallow Moses'-basket, which the young men carried
on two forked poles inserted at the side. Tired and intoxicated
by the fresh air she slept, with her head on her right shoulder.
Occasionally, when there was a jerk, she would open her eyes,
but seeing above her the green branches, the sky and a rosy
glow, she would close them again, and thinking that she was
dreaming she smiled the delicate smile of a sick child who is
recovering.

After some time the upward slope ended. They passed
through thick forests and the road was wider and gentler.
Here they began to meet, in groups, people from other places.
There were seriously sick ones who, loaded like sacks on to
horses, moaned huskily and rolled their eyes. There were also
mad and raving ones, whom their relations supported and paci-
fied.

Old Bademlićka walked ahead of her own folk, pushed her
way between the people, and not looking at anybody recited
her rosary in a whisper. The bearers could hardly keep up with
her. Twice they rested in a beech wood beside the road.
During lunch they spread a brown rug on the grass and placed
the sick girl on it. She stretched her numb legs and cramped
form as much as she could. She took fright when she saw her
mother's feet beside her, bare, bruised and blood-stained from
the unaccustomed journey. But the old woman quickly drew her

feet in beneath her wide trouser legs, and the little girl, happily
bewildered by so many new things around her, at once forgot
that. Everything was new, unusual and delightful: the thick
dark forest grass, the heavy beeches with toadstools like shelves
on their silvery bark, the birds which dropped on to the
horses' oat-sacks, and the wide view with the bright sky and
long oval-shaped clouds which sailed slowly along. And when
the horse shook its head and the birds flew up, scared, around
it, the little girl although tired and sleepy had to laugh, long and
softly. She watched the lads eating slowly and seriously, and
in that too there was something funny and merry. And she herself ate with relish. She stretched herself out on her rug as
much as she could. Spreading out the cool grass with her hand
she noticed a flower, called 'granny's ear', tiny and brilliant
scarlet, close to the dark soil as if lost. She cried out softly
from excitement. The old woman, who had dozed off from
weariness, awoke and plucked it for her. The little one looked
at it and smelt it for a long time, holding it on her palm, and
then pressed it on her cheek, and when she felt how velvety and
cool it was she closed her eyes from delight.

   In the early evening they arrived at Olovo. Around the ruins
of the monastery and the vaulted pool from which could be
heard dully the warm water of the Spring of Our Lady falling,
there was a whole fairground of people. Fires burned, there was
roasting, boiling and eating. The majority were sleeping on the
level ground. In one shed was a place for the wealthier and
upper-class people. Here the Bademlić family installed themselves. Both women quickly fell fast asleep. But the little girl
passed the whole night as if in some half-dream; she gazed
through the window at the stars above the dark forest, so many
stars that she had never seen as many. She listened to the
voices, which did not cease to murmur the whole night around
the fires, and so she would drift down into sleep; but then a
horse's neighing or the freshness of the night would waken her.
Listening again to the rustling and the voices, she was unable

to collect her senses at all and to discover when she was dreaming and when she was awake.

The next day in the early morning they went to the spring.

First one entered a low, half-dark room, in which one undressed. The floor-boards were wet and rotten. Along the walls stood wooden benches on which were the clothes that were left. From there one descended, down three steep wooden steps, to a larger and somewhat brighter room in which was the pool. Everything was of stone. The roof was stone, vaulted, and high up near the top were little round openings through which a strange light fell in shafts. Footsteps echoed and the stone arched roof magnified and sent back every noise, even the slightest. The rushing sound of the water rebounded from the arches and, multiplied and magnified, filled the whole space so that one had to shout when speaking. And that shout was again split and doubled beneath the vaults. Evaporation made breathing difficult. From the walls and arches seeped water beneath which a green stalactite was clinging, as in caves.

The water fell in a thick stream out of a stone gutter. It was warm, clear, full of little silvery bubbles; it spilled over the stone pool, and there, from the grey slabs, it acquired a greenish colour.

They bathed in turn, men, then women. When the women's turn came there began a pushing, arguing and calling out. Some were dressed, and only took off their shoes and waded in the water, which came to above their knees; others had undressed right to their chemises. Barren women crouched, up to their necks in the water, and prayed with their eyes closed. Some caught the water from the stream in their palms and rinsed their throats, ears and nostrils. And each was so occupied with her prayer and with the thought of recovery that nobody recoiled from anyone, as if they did not see each other. They jogged one another a little, and quarrelled over places, but immediately forgot their dispute and each other again.

Old Bademlićka and her sister-in-law led the girl to the

water. Even though all were in a state of ecstasy and each was occupied with herself, yet they all made room, for rich and distinguished people never and nowhere lose their precedence.

Cramped as she is, the girl trembles and fears the water and the people. But she gradually lets herself down deeper and deeper into the water, as if she wishes to hide herself. And if they had not been supporting her under her armpits she would have sat down on the bottom. Even so, the water came to beneath her chin. Never in her life had she seen so much water or heard so many voices and strange echoes. Only occasionally, when she would dream that she was well, that she could walk and run, had she dreamed she was bathing with other children in some water or other, and that there were dancing about her body like this, now, these innumerable, bright, tiny bubbles. She was exhilarated. She closed her eyes and rapidly inhaled the warm steam from the water. As if from a greater and greater distance she heard the voices of the women around her. She felt something tickling her eyes. She pressed her eyelids together more firmly but the tickling did not stop. Finally with difficulty she opened her eyes. Through one of those round holes in the arched roof a shaft of sunlight penetrated and fell on her face. In the brightness the watery steam flickered and rose like fine dust, green, blue and golden. The sick girl followed it with her gaze. Suddenly she began to shake, and jerked a few times, then began, with an effort, to raise herself out of the water. Amazed, her mother and aunt began to let go of her, supporting her more and more lightly. And the cramped and paralysed girl suddenly straightened up, as never before, then let go the hands which were supporting her at the side, and still slightly stooping began to walk slowly and uncertainly like a small child. She stretched out her arms. On the thin wet chemise her little breasts showed, with their dark red tips. Between her heavy eyelashes there flashed a moist gleam. Her full lips stretched into a sudden dull and sensual smile. She raised her head, and gazing upwards, high up into that shaft of light, she suddenly shouted with some unexpectedly clear and penetrating voice:

'There he is! He's coming down on the clouds. Jesus, Jesus! Ah!'

13   From the book *On the Road*

PETAR ŠEGEDIN

The young man had already eaten his meal; he busied himself with contemplation of me. A new guest cut short my state of composure: a man of medium height, with a firm, compact body and a similarly compactly formed swarthy face, with a bristly brush-shaped moustache just slightly greying. He moved energetically, in a good, somewhat worn suit, and found himself unexpectedly by our table; and as if by the way, just, just so much as to carry out a formality, asked for permission to sit down. Before my neighbour had said anything he had already sat down and had begun to call the waiter loudly. We did not interest him; one sensed, however, that he knew we were watching him, but it was as though he were superior to that. The waiter could not come immediately, and he was visibly getting ruffled. At last the waiter approached and told him which dishes were left, but he did not wish to listen to him; on the contrary, he obstinately asked for the *carte*, let the *carte* be brought to him, he eats *à la carte*. The waiter brought him the menu, the guest began to argue with him, and when for the third time he had been told that he had arrived late, he made a dismissive movement with his hand in a superior fashion, continuing to peer at the sheet of paper, probably reading and learning by heart everything that could have been got in the hotel that day. Finally he was given the same dish that had been served to me too.

My young neighbour became calmer, as if the new guest had helped him to feel at ease: he glanced at me and now, already, obviously wished to establish contact. Our feelings were the same towards the new guest. I remained passive, and the young man began to feel that he was alone: signs of embarrassment

were again to be traced, glints of discreet reproach appeared
in his blue eyes. One more dark experience in his life; and he
began to close up. I clearly recognised that failure of mine.
Insignificant, perhaps, in the development of that personality,
but perhaps it was one of those moments which decide . . . In
order to save myself from an uneasy feeling I turned my
attention to the new guest. His fleshy face, occupied in feeding,
imposed on me a direct comparison with the face of the young
man.

The new guest was completely engrossed in his food. With
visible pleasure he examined the plate, forks, spoon, knife and
glasses, and evidently he did not like the knife; he put it to one
side and drew out his little pocket knife, opened it, cleaned the
blade with his thumb and forefinger, and began to carve his
piece of meat with it. Not by one sign did he disclose that he
cared about his surroundings: enclosed and surrounded by *his*
interests, in his gestures, in *his* love for everything *his*, he
aroused in me the fear which all people have aroused with
whom I have established that contact is impossible somewhere
on the human line. His systematic and definite manner in his
movements, in his indifference towards his entire surroundings,
gave its expression to that face: a complete man, but what
kind of a man! . . .

I turned my glance to my other neighbour, but he was
looking towards the window. He wanted to go: the sun and
open spaces were calling him, but some kind of persistence,
probably lazy, held him back on his chair.

On one side a complete man, and on the other a new
traveller into life . . .

14　From the novel *The Evil Springtide*

MIHAILO LALIĆ

Often we were in the violet-coloured hollows below the teacher's house. Under the shelter of little shrubs like maquis a bit of grass still remained, and the goats busied themselves with the hawthorn shoots. And I felt good there—in that vicinity, secret and almost painful because of my longing and unbelievable dreamings—in the same air that Vidra breathed, looking at the trees and the bends in the river which she looked at.

That part seemed to me exceptional in the world, and I don't know how much I admired Jasikić the teacher for having planted the fruit trees and put up the fences. In all this, one thing couldn't be imagined without the other, as if there was nothing to add to it or to take away: the red roof and the window-panes which glitter above garlands of greenery full of beehives and apples; and where water spurts out in a dense white cascade from the deep veins of the earth.

But out of all this Branko only liked the apples. He knocked them down with a catapult, and they would roll to the fence, bruised, juicy and fragrant. He prided himself on their beauty as if he had created it himself, and it never occurred to him that this method was not allowed and that one should restrain oneself, because he did not knock them down to eat them but to give them to others. He only liked to be doing something, to be achieving something, to occupy his hands.

They were restless, self-willed hands, which had, as it were, some separate brain of their own, and they never left time for thought to catch up with them and prevent them from doing what they were hankering after. His pop-guns and blow-pipes of elder caused much headache to Jasikić the teacher.

And then he made a little water-mill on the stream and it was said that his hands created everything that his eyes saw; but he made even more than that: some suspended gutters out of which, through a pierced groove, little drops sound at regular intervals, like a clock, dropping on to a small tin sheet placed beneath.

I had hoped that there would develop here a talented engineer, but nothing came of it. He did not last out even a month in the secondary school: he quarrelled with the town children about a ball, drove them into a corner by the mosque and, attacking their place of refuge, smashed the windows of some shopkeeper. He had drawn Luka's Nenad and some others also into that squabble—they expelled them all under paragraph 42, as if they had been looking forward to that rumpus. He did not turn bitter about it, and it was as though he sighed with relief. 'Now I am a free citizen,' he said, and with this he consoled others, too, who for various reasons had to leave school.

But I remained still longer without freedom, and doubly so. And that autumn, when many cattle were perishing in the markets where nobody wished to buy them, seemed beautiful to me. Every day I saw Vidra—in the evening, when we were returning from school. Fear of darkness crowded us together into a group that covered its kilometres and shortened the way with a song. One night some job detained us in the town; I think that it was actually a job of hers—some shopping or other—and we were late, she and Jug Jeremić and I.

The moon soon went down. A clear and cool night with the rustling of fallen leaves. The Lim, shallow, had settled down beneath the bank and become quiet, full of stars. The hearths in the villages across the Lim shone as if they were stars too, and the dogs, satiated—for there was slaughtering everywhere—quietly made their presence known, to break the silence. Then Jug dropped in at his uncle's place to pass the night there, for it was nearer for him like that, and left us alone. I think that he did this intentionally, but we have never spoken about it.

Then—it was as if my voice deserted me. Numb in my mouth and turned to wood, my tongue lay dead. And from then on I said nothing, nor did she. We walked and walked through that starry night—the stones talked with the trees around us, in various voices, and I listened to my heart hammering madly and was afraid that she would hear it too, but I could do nothing to calm it down.

At last we reached the well in front of their house. And she said:

'Goodbye!'

It was in a soft voice, so similar to the murmuring sounds that even now I am surprised that I have been able to recall what was scarcely to be distinguished from that soft rustling with which a leaf separates from a branch when it falls off.

Memory is a strange thing, and I who have forgotten many a sound of thunder, even now, it seems, hear that murmur repeated again and again. And even if there will not be another meeting, I shall never, never let that moment at least go from me—as long as I can revive it like this.

15   From the novel *Silences*

MEŠA SELIMOVIĆ

One day passes, two, three, I don't know how many, and I'm waiting for something to happen. I am sure that it will happen —some joy, love, anything that is not the morose greyness of day and night. It's strange, I say to myself—haven't I come to a standstill too suddenly? The whirl of war has stopped all at once, and now I cannot adjust my step.

Inevitably I feel like a homeless man. That is not altogether bad, I have no obligations nor restrictions, only it's somewhat empty. It's all one to me where I'll go off to when I finish work. I have always wished for that complete liberty, but I don't go off anywhere, I don't take advantage of a single opportunity, nor do I really know what they are. We walk without any object, we look for each other, and when we find each other we talk about the war.

Not a single place is ours, we don't know how to take possession of one; it's as if we are about to go away somewhere. In the café there is a wasteland of uniforms, of sheepskin coats, sharp odour, smoke, loud conversations; an ostentatiously joyless throng in which one feels that the terrain is neither ours nor someone else's. And we despise it, we don't move our feet out of the way in their boots and heavy clogs, we look from aloft on the waiters who drag themselves along unwillingly, almost with disgust. And they despise us, with no bowing of their back, with eyebrow raised, dirty tunic, absent-mindedness. We can't find our feet yet, neither we nor they. The waiter is somewhere far away in his thoughts, cut off from us, staring at the large window which is shaking because of a tank passing.

'Coffee,' I asked again.

'Yes, sir. I heard.'

Irony in the professional politeness, scorn which he scarcely hides. His eyes are age-old: through them have passed thousands of people, and each is assessed in a tiny part of a second. We new ones, we are assessed all together, it was not worth sorting us out individually.

The coffee is bad, luke-warm, unpalatable.

'You haven't a better coffee?'

The waiter glowed with happiness:

'We haven't. Another one, please?'

'No.'

'Well,' asks Duško, 'what have you been doing these three days?'

'Is it really three days already?'

'It's gone quickly for you?'

'It hasn't gone quickly.'

I tell about the 'weasel'; he laughs merrily. He asks:

'Is she ugly?'

'She's not ugly.'

'Well, why, then? Young, pretty, why didn't you stay?'

'She's no longer that girl of former times.'

'Precisely because of that. Now you're more necessary to her.'

'I don't like pity.'

'But imagine if you had married before the war?'

'How would it be?'

'I don't know.'

I wait for him to tell everything, but he becomes silent. I don't know what he is hiding, and I don't want to ask. Better thus. I don't like my own or other people's confessions.

Then I tell him about the editorial office. The editor had received me so cordially that I had already got the idea that there was a misunderstanding. But there wasn't any misunderstanding, he knew who I was, we used to meet and knew each other during the war, but not so as to account for such great cordiality. Anyway, so I thought; he didn't: he knew me

so thoroughly that I was scared. Indeed, he knew everybody.
While we were sitting in the office many people came in, as
though into a café; nobody announced himself. And he called
each one by his name, clapped him on the shoulder, enquired
about acquaintances, and the people were embarrassed
although I did not know why.

He slapped me on the arms, exclaimed with pleasure,
shouted Ah, and Oh, and I'm delighted, and Where have you
been so long? and then by telephone ordered two teas, rather
strong. He asked me:

'Do you still like pretty strong tea?'

I've never liked even to see tea, either pretty strong or
pretty weak, and I say, apologising:

'I prefer coffee.'

'Coffee,' he ordered, disappointed. And a little surprised, it
seemed to me. But he regained his balance:

'Well, how is it in your Užice?'

'I'm not from Užice.'

'Oh yes, from Kragujevac.'

I was not from Kragujevac either.

'Oh, I see,' he continued, already a little nervily, although
he kept smiling. 'I'm glad that we shall be working together.
At last you'll be able to work at your own subject.'

With terror I wait to hear what is my subject. He did not
leave me long in uncertainty.

'Economics, I believe?'

This is my subject just as much as Sanskrit. But I keep
silent. If I rebel again it will turn out that we don't know each
other at all, or that he is under a complete delusion, I don't
know which is worse. And I look at him stupidly, trying to keep
the normal expression of my face. I even kept smiling, though
with an effort, thinking that it's not always easy with people
who do know everything. But it seems that I exaggerated in
my endeavour to convince him that everything was all right,
and he began to look at me suspiciously.

'Or isn't it?'

I knew that that curt question referred to my subject, but it sounded threatening. I was in a state of torment: to admit or not to admit? I answered curtly, according to his model:

'Language.'

'Russian?' he asked with a final hope.

'French.'

'Completed university course?'

'No.'

'Oh, well. Good, we'll see.'

Duško laughed at my story.

'You've invented it all,' he said.

'Not absolutely everything. Let's say half.'

He laughed again, with less justification now, and longer than was necessary. And when he became silent he looked at the ashtray and said vaguely:

'Well, well.'

'What: well, well?'

'Nothing. It seems to me that you're dissatisfied. Perhaps you were expecting something different.'

'I was expecting to be the governor of the National Bank.'

We burst into laughter, but I had a feeling of unease. I felt sore, as if he had come upon me in a disgraceful act. But in fact I was not thinking about that, I was not resenting my undefined position, which might be only modest, I hadn't even any plans or wishes, it was all the same to me; what I should do with the job and what it would do with me it was absurd even to imagine. If I had been expecting confidence, that's natural— I believed in myself, like all who haven't tried their hands at anything. All doors are open to us, all wishes can be realised, all opportunities are within reach, it is only necessary to wish, and I do wish. It's all one where I shall start from, somewhere there will burst out this accumulated sensitivity which I can hardly cope with because I don't yet know what to subordinate

it to. What I'll have done will be necessary to someone, someone will stop in front of it and look at me wonderingly: really, is
that your work? I don't yet know what sort of work it is, but
whatever it may be it will be fine.

Duško looks at me, smiles in order to dispel a possible un-
easiness because of his question.

'What are you thinking about?'

'He somehow deprived me of my personality. I felt as
though I have no roots or settled place.'

'Whom are you talking about?'

'About the editor.'

'Very important.'

'Of course.'

'I mean, what the editor says. Shall we go somewhere?'

'Where?'

'Anywhere. To drink, to be crazy.'

'Why?'

'Oh, just like that. If you want to.'

'I don't. I don't feel any need at all.'

'Then everything's all right.'

'Everything's all right.'

16 *The Belated Visitor*

NIKOLA ŠOP

He entered just at a moment when the guests in the drawing-room had fallen silent. They all heard his arrival. The muffled grating of the lock. And the dull sound of steps in the deep carpet.

Now he would enter. Already one hears a coat being taken off and a clicking of buttons. And the passing of a comb through hair. Yes, now he has certainly glanced at himself once more in the mirror.

And see, he is coming in.

But he is still not here. What is he doing? He is already suspect to everyone. Is he searching the coats? He's looking for notes. Jewellery, secret letters. Or traces of scent left in the depths of women's hats are intoxicating him.

The visitor looks round, in fear. He listens. Now, in this moment, he must complete that secret task. For otherwise he will be discovered in the act, caught. Terrible. The obliging host, or some guest feeling at home, might appear to see what he was doing and to bring him in. To bring him in, unprepared like that. He would stand in the midst of the company, all benumbed, flustered and completely naked.

Now he must, he must go in. The secret task is completed; the decision is made. It is as though he quickly removes something from his face and flings it into some secret chest, and from another, again, extracts something and draws it on to his face. So. Now he is calm. Once again he goes to the mirror. He no longer recognises himself.

None of the guests knows what the belated visitor had done. But each had done the same when he was putting aside his hat and coat. He is silent about it now, for if the secret should be disclosed one would ruthlessly strip from another's face the mask which he had stealthily put on in the hall.

The belated visitor entered at last, smiling.

17 *The Guest—Bringer of Fear*

NIKOLA ŠOP

What was in that man's face, that they were all afraid of him, were avoiding him, and secretly hated him? Already from a distance each guest had recognised him by his step. And in a moment, already he had burst into the drawing-room, without discarding either his coat or his hat in the entrance hall—he left everything somewhere in a corner of the drawing-room.

'What boldness! What barbarism!' angrily whispered the visitors. And nothing more, for he would have been able to hear.

Immediately afterwards all began to compete in approaching him as close as possible. In overwhelming him with words as flattering as possible. In expressing admiration with a smile, the pressure of a hand, and with eyes tear-filled from emotion.

And then: running up, offers, bringing of the best food and drink, which were kept only for him. And finally unanimous and thunderous acknowledgement that he only was worthy to sit at the head of the table.

But out of all the smiles, bowing and admiration were issuing a hidden fear, and an aversion towards that man.

Why do they hate him so? Why is his face so bright to them that they shield their eyes? Why do they tremble before him from hidden terror?

Because he has come among them—without a mask.

The Absent-minded Guest

NIKOLA ŠOP

In the midst of the liveliest conversation, which he was leading, the words suddenly stuck in his throat and became obscure.

Somebody's eyes were observing him relentlessly and horrified.

He sensed a faintness, a whirling, and a darker and darker mistiness before him, and—he collapsed into unconsciousness. He only heard, still, the alarm raised, a muffled hustling, the resonant fall of a glass, and then—peace.

Then, as if he were emerging from the deep, nearer and nearer to some light surface, nearer and nearer to brightness, he began to breathe and to sip a stream of something refreshing. He nervously opened his eyes.

Over him many faces were bent. Arms were firmly supporting him. And someone's voice was heard:

'Sir, what was it that happened to you? Take more water. You will be fresh again.'

He stood up, with a smile thanked them and begged them to excuse him for disturbing the company by an unfortunate accident.

Although they all pressed him and cordially begged him to stay, nevertheless he took leave of them all and went home. He had to do so, for otherwise he would have experienced a complete breakdown.

Resting in an armchair at his table, he could not wonder enough at himself.

That he should be so forgetful, so incautious! He, who had always been enigmatic to everybody and always attractive just because of that mysteriousness of his.

No, he still cannot get over it at all. In vain the consoling words which he speaks to himself. In vain all the delusions that nobody had noticed his ill-fated absent-mindedness. Perhaps they hadn't, for why—when he had emerged from unconsciousness—were they questioning him:

'Sir, what was it that happened to you?'

So nobody had any idea. Nobody even suspected.

But only one guest. Only that man who had been still and silent the whole time. Even yet, before his eyes, is his keen and penetrating gaze. That gaze because of which he had fainted. And that horrible whisper which will persecute him for ever.

The whisper: 'Poor wretch, I've seen through you. I found, forgotten in the entrance hall—your mask.'

19 From an article *A City with a Famous Past*

from the magazine *Review*

History shows that already about the year 1000 Zagreb must have been a proper little town, for by a decision of king Ladislav as early as the 11th century it was chosen as the seat of a Christian bishopric, one of the first Catholic bishoprics in the Balkans. In one medieval document of the year 1094 the name of Zagreb is mentioned—in the Latin form 'Zagrabia'—and thus Zagreb received its thousand-year-old certificate of baptism.

Some centuries later, well fortified militarily, Zagreb played its most significant role for the history of Europe. Directly below it, and in the area around it, the centuries-long Ottoman incursion into Europe was halted and crushed. The Turks besieged Zagreb several times, but her strong fortifications—a part of the walls is visible still today—they never succeeded in overcoming. Even today the tradition is maintained that in memory of one retreat of the Turks, every day at 2 p.m. a special bell sounds from the Cathedral.

20 From an article *November in Belgrade*

from the magazine *Review*

When on 20th October 1944 units of the National-Liberation Army liberated Belgrade, there were fewer than 300,000 inhabitants in it—fewer than had lived in it before the war. Today Belgrade, with a wider area, has over a million inhabitants, which means that every twentieth Yugoslav lives in this city.

Immediately after the liberation the people of Belgrade were up against enormous difficulties. In the half-ruined city there were not the basic conditions necessary for the lives of a hundred thousand people. Through the exceptional verve not only of the inhabitants of Belgrade but of the whole community the first difficulties were overcome. The town grew and spread, and today it is the largest and finest since its origin. All the principal blocks of flats in Belgrade have been erected since the liberation. Almost with the speed of a film new quarters have been springing up. What only a few years ago was regarded as the farthest periphery of the city is today modern settlements; children's playgrounds, schools, medical welfare centres, cinemas, shopping centres arise along with the new housing estates.

On the right bank of the Danube, across the Sava, a new town has sprung up. On the marshy and sandy ground youth brigades from the whole country laid the foundations for New Belgrade in 1948.

New boulevards cut across New Belgrade. Institutions of which one thought little at the beginning are springing up in an ever greater number. Hotels, modern shopping centres, halls for sports, medical institutions planned according to all the principles of contemporary architecture are today already a reality.

21 From an article *Titograd*

from the magazine *Review*

Only since 1946, when Titograd began to spring up on the ruins of Podgorica, has the town begun to acquire the contours of a modern settlement. It had all the conditions for becoming the principal town of Montenegro. It is situated at the inter-section of routes which lead towards the sea and into the interior of the country. The Titograd airport is connected by airlines with all the larger centres in the land.

If Titograd itself, as a new town, has no interesting ancient monuments, its surroundings in that respect are very attractive. Twelve kilometres away is one of the oldest fortifications in the country—Medun—which dates from the 4th century B.C. The Greeks erected it, on a small hill. But the greatest attrac-tion of Titograd is Duklja, three kilometres from the town. This settlement was built at the time of the Roman Emperor Diocletian, at the place where the Zeta flows into the Morača. To this day are preserved the foundations of many buildings, certain fragments, items of sculpture and an array of interesting objects of artists' crafts.

22   From an article *The Belgrade–Bar Railroad**

from the magazine *Review*

The Belgrade–Bar railway line, which, by the shortest route, connects almost half of Yugoslavia (49% of the territory with nine and a half million inhabitants) with the Adriatic Sea—and this means with the world, with world markets and the world scientific and technical revolution—must be classed among exceptional projects not only in Yugoslavia but in Europe also. It passes through the most beautiful and hitherto inaccessible regions of the country, through 253 tunnels, over 100 bridges —which means 100 deep, wild and exceptionally beautiful canyons (the bridge over the River Mala is 200 metres high) in a total length of over 14 kilometres, to emerge within reach of the sea, between the mountain massifs of Durmitor and Prokletije, at a height of 1,036 metres; and then abruptly—like an eagle in a curving downward swoop—it descends to only 30 metres above sea level. And in one spurt it speeds across the lake of Skadar, in whose age-old silence pelicans hatch their young, and comes to a halt on the loveliest and sunniest shore of the Adriatic Sea.

* The construction of this railway is not yet completed.

23 From the novel *Perfumes, Gold and Frankincense*

'Gold, Frankincense and Myrrh'

SLOBODAN NOVAK

I caught sight of Draga on that same spot at which I had left her so many days before. She was standing on the deck, beside that really exquisite suitcase, as if she had just got out of a tram and stopped for a moment at the tram-stop beneath the chestnut trees. I think that that suitcase is the most beautiful and most expensive thing that we have. An object. And why we have a suitcase, precisely, so superb and fine, God knows! We scarcely use it, and so many other things one hasn't, dear Lord! Draga is the sort of woman who would have to have everything of hers in the style of the suitcase, and over and above that a whole lot of miscellaneous trifles and objects and three loads of treasure. There is not on the whole deck a person so tastefully dressed, and there wouldn't even be such a one if the late *Queen Mary* herself had sailed in. Ah, what are we to do? I know it's no use saying anything!

Draga and I weren't addressing each other in the way that this is done, across the heads of all the people, by waving, stretching out our necks, rearing up on to our toes. We only gave each other a smile, and I—it's true—went over there to the boat itself, to beneath the deck on which she was standing. I did not want to wait at the foot of the gangway. I was looking at her from below. All right—I was, but anyway she knew how to behave with good taste, she pressed her skirt with her knees against the ship's rail and asked, approximately, in that scrimmage: 'How are things up there?' And I said, with my head and shoulders, that everything was all right on the whole; and now I immediately wanted to ask her how things were up there, for Zagreb is 'up', just as Madonna's house is, and for us everything is always somewhere 'up'; but I probably made an incoherent gesture and Draga only nodded her head, thinking that I was doing just anything, like that, on account of this bloody audience around us, who always expect the people coming from the boat on to the shore, and vice versa, to announce something to each other hastily, as if it were the end of the world. Still, she seemed to me slightly enigmatic, and I repeated a few times in succession the signs of questioning, with my eyebrows, but to this she answered something like: 'There are no problems, please don't torment me!' But in a moment she was giggling again, there like that, with shadows around her mouth and across her nose, and since I did not know my wife, for one can never get to know women, I resigned myself to waiting for the smell of her skin, by which I usually draw my conclusions best. Coming down the gangway towards me was my golden conserve, from which the label had dropped off, and I, hungry in every way, was only waiting to know which and what kind of juices to extract when the contents should be declared.

'How are things?' I say, and kiss her on the cheek and take the suitcase. 'Children well? Everybody well?'

She only confirmed with a mumble. She smelled of the distances which stretch between this morning's sunrise and this noontide. But of personal scents I could smell nothing in this conventional contact in front of the crew of the boat and the shore, and in front of the citizens of the town.

We dug ourselves out of that jam at the foot of the gangway and entered the little procession which, leaving the quay, was moving beneath the town walls and hauling a whole shop of articles that cannot be found on the island counters. Draga had a kind of broken, slackened step like long-legged marsh birds, and told only half about everything, but was fairly satisfied although up there everything was allegedly somehow different; and all the formalities were in order—greetings, health, messages and so on, and then at the end she said we must hurry so that Erminia would not be waiting. I said that there was no Erminia at home and that Madonna knew about my going out, and I began to submit to her a brief sketch of our future style of living and of our partial emancipation, but she from the beginning hastened her step, slightly panicky, and wouldn't let herself be reasoned with, and on the way to the house one couldn't embark on anything seriously with her any more. Only when hurrying up the steps to the little piazza did she rebuke me, breathlessly:

'You ought not to have done that to me! If it was hard for you you should have told me, and I wouldn't have gone away anywhere. What does it look like, now, that she's in the house alone?'

'Very important! She won't steal anything!' I snapped angrily, dragging that suitcase at a lively pace up the steep slopes and the flights of steps. 'What are you so afraid of? She won't run away to the graveyard!'

She did not answer, however, and did not even look round at me any more, but slightly sideways, as though she were hiding herself, she sailed rather gracefully along by the walls towards the house.

When I arrived after her she was already wrapped in her housefrock. At first, in her haste, she had forgotten her hat, then she took that off too, although that, I think, is usually taken off first. She ruffled her stiff perm a little, and went into Madonna's room, saying quite normally and calmly:

'How are you this morning? They told me that you were calling me. Do you want some cool tea, just a little, eh?'

Madonna was silent. She was silent, silent.

Draga had confused her by her calmness, but it was not clear whether she had won as well. She still busied herself a little about the chest of drawers, and then went out of the room as busily as she had entered. Coming out, she covered her mouth with her hands in panic, and began to roll her eyes, wondering what was going to happen. Then she turned to the cooking, for lunchtime had already passed and I had counted on the new cook that day so I had only prepared everything, lit the fire and—got hungry.

Several times already I had asked her how things were up there; this interested me indescribably, but there was no way of getting any real answer, or at least some tiny morsel for the sake of orientation, or to enjoy. So I moved up to her from behind her back and threatened that I would cut off her head if she did not answer three questions, which ran, all three: How are things up there?

At this she quivered, from a kind of sudden shudder, and without turning her eyes away from her task she said, at first confused:

'I don't know. Everything is somehow different.' Then she reflected a little and glanced at me sideways, and, ostensibly more cheerfully, said: 'Different somehow, really. Everything's different'—as if she wished to make her first word, that had been so serious, lighter.

I wondered: different—how? Somehow? What does different mean? Different from what? Different from before? Different from what she had been imagining that it would be? What does different mean?

'And you yourself are different!'

'Yes. I, too.'

24 From the novel *The Holidays*

ALEKSANDAR VUČO

At the end of June, when we had received our marks and both knew that we had passed into the sixth form, Ladislav invited me to supper. Their flat was situated in the central building in a kind of rectangular tower, which stood out above the hospital pavilions. I smoothed my hair and rang. In a little half-dark hall white officers' tunics, brought out to wake up from their winter sleep, are hanging on a peg. Opposite, an oval mirror in a heavy gilt frame. A smell of carbolic. Ladislav appeared, nervous, a little shy. He opened one of four doors, and indicated with his hand that I was to enter (a gesture which came to a stop between exaggerated politeness and comradely cordiality). I entered a spacious room. Lowered roller blinds protect it from the sun, midway from its zenith to setting. Dark walls, covered with violet-coloured wallpaper. Pictures and photographs. The furniture hidden beneath heavy table-cloths, covers, embroidered table runners, loose covers.

In the middle of the room stood his mother. Small, with a very narrow face. Her greying hair, combed back, retained the elasticity of life. An absent-minded automatic movement of her hand when she shook hands with me. On a velvet ribbon round her neck a cameo in a gold setting. A white Venetian shawl thrown across her narrow shoulders. Her bosom hidden. A type which one meets in books.

She smiled at me with a blue glance, a little sly, and said, uttering the words in a rapid rhythm:

'I was just reading Voltaire. Imagine, children, he forbade walks, cut down people's portions of food ... Ah! You are that Dragan about whom Ladislav has talked so much to me. Stand beside him, please. Come along! Ladja, please, you too, only for a moment. For me to see something.'

She took us by our arms, led us to the middle of the room, and placed our backs together.

'You're taller than my Ladja by two centimetres. Who would have thought it? But on the other hand he's broader—broader in the shoulders. See, look in the mirror, see for yourselves. And how much, too!' she said, with unconcealed triumph. Almost maliciously.

She then drew us near to the window.

'Your eyes are lighter, speckled. His dark, after his father. And much deeper, much deeper . . . My handsome Ladislav!'

We sat down in armchairs with broad backs, around a circular table heaped up with little boxes with incrustations of mother-of-pearl, and family albums bound in velvet, with ostentatiously large silver clasps. This lasted only a few minutes. With the noisiness of a restless child she jumped up, went over to the piano, lifted the lid.

'Do you like music?' And she began to play a Chopin mazurka.

She was leaving on me an impression as if she was drunk or naked.

She stopped playing. She turned round.

'You know, I'm Polish, my father was a manufacturer of vinegar, or yeast—I no longer know of what exactly . . . There wasn't a rich man in Warsaw then who didn't court me. But why am I telling you this? Oh yes . . . something induced me to lead a double life, a flight of steps which led away further, higher than fate had decreed. Girlish dreams? Gape—let me tell you! I married an officer—against my father's will. He was terrible, my papa Tadija. I ran away with Milivoj. He was then in a military deputation, as handsome as St. George. For a long time we were happy. And . . .'

Waves of scarlet alternated with the pallor on Ladja's face.

'Excuse me, mama, but this doesn't interest Dragan,' he said resolutely. 'Allow me to show him the photographs.'

We went off along the walls. She, hurt, continued the Chopin.

In slender frames: horses. Stallions for breeding, mares with foal, a series of the firsts in the Derby at Epsom during the last ten years, steeplechases, collections of jockeys, photographs of small thin men with dedications and autographs, diplomas with seals, trainers, racecourses, stables, pedigrees. On shelves in the left-hand corner: horse-shoes (one of gold), spurs, jockeys' sashes, crossed riding-whips; opposite, pictures of officers, merry groups on outings, manoeuvres, riding in the ring, captains' pips, drinking parties. On one wall, completely alone, a large portrait in colour—her Milivoj. Erect, with dark blue eyes, sabre-shaped eyebrows.

I was dumbfounded. Everything together was pressing down upon me a burden of symbolic suggestions, with extra-ordinarily sinister force, sumptuous and unbearable in the process of the conquest of my mind.

Into the room there came a young girl, perhaps a year or two older than I. A black skirt to her ankles, which were tied firmly into deep black lace-up boots. Around her waist, slender as that of a wasp, a wide belt of black patent leather. A white blouse of the cut of a man's shirt. Deep, deep black plaits about the nape of her neck, the sharp slash of a centre parting. Eyes neither green nor blue. From them spring out long curving eyelashes. Cheeks of dark wax.

'You can go across into the dining-room.' She addressed everyone in the room. 'Supper is served.'

'Let me introduce you.' Ladislav drew me forward by the arm. 'Vanda, my sister—Dragan, my best friend.'

'So that's you,' she said in a voice in which there floated something strange and dark. 'And I had thought . . .'

'What had you thought?' Ladislav asked gaily.

'That your friend was different . . .'

She turned and went towards the door of the dining-room.

Their mother still went on playing, giving us a sign with her head that we need not wait for her.

We drank chocolate, ate a sweet rice dish sprinkled with cinnamon, and some little cakes in the shape of many-pointed stars, moistened with honey and essence of vanilla. I felt again that something dark, strange, disturbing was hovering around Vanda and pleading for mutual understanding. She told us about a little cat, dirty, still blind, which she had found in front of a cellar window. 'Mitsi, Mitsi!' she called, bent down and picked up from the floor a black kitten. With it in her hand she stood up, and asked me suddenly:

'So next year at this time you too enter the Academy? Cavalry or artillery?'

I answered that I'd like to very much, but that I doubted whether my father would allow me to.

'From my birth he's been preparing me for a business man. I've got to inherit his export business,' I added, filling every word with bitter irony.

She placed the kitten on her shoulder, lowered her thick eye-lashes and said something about it being seen that a little of my mother's milk still remained on my lips, and that I must wipe it away as soon as possible, because my life belonged only to me.

'Vanda!' Ladislav admonished her.

She tossed her head defiantly and went over to the open window at the far end of the room.

A mauvish light lay on things, on her hair, on the roofs of the hospital pavilions. Like a coat of fresh paint. In the poplars the shattered mirror of the sinking sun.

She returned and sat down again at the table. Her body was developing, warm, supple. She could not draw near me without my beginning to tremble. She was taking over the driving force in me. She dominated my thoughts.

'You must be energetic. Tell your father that it's a question of life or death. If I had listened to papa and mama I'd now be singing do-re-mi in a music school. Let's educate our parents!'

25   From the short story *The Birthday*

ANTUN ŠOLJAN

We had been here long ago, and had promised that we would
return. Nobody had kept the promise, like a thousand other
promises made in a state of elation, forgotten in the following
calm moment. Promises for which it is always too late. We have
always prided ourselves on not keeping them, and on the fact
that we live changeable in a changeable world.

Nobody ever regretted that we had nowhere to return to.

The house was discovered by Marijan, a friend of my youth,
about whom I cannot think, even today, entirely without
emotion. He was a vagabond, a loafer, free and cynical in his
language and actions; for nothing did he show any respect,
nothing did he love more than himself, nothing bound him.
He fled from every yoke which people would try to force upon
him. He evaded family ties, long-term business contracts,
permanent friends and long-lasting love affairs. He was always
more ready to take up with numerous unstable women than one
reliable one. He was always travelling, trailing around on trains
and ships, rather than dwelling in a definite city, in his own
home. He hated things which aroused in him the desire to
possess them.

We seldom saw each other, but our meetings, in various
places and in unexpected circumstances, were always filled
with some mystical significance for us both. There was always
something weighty about them, some holiday, festive feeling,
as if something extraordinary were happening, something
which would have far-reaching consequences not only for our
lives but also for all the people around us; but from outside
those meetings looked perfectly natural, logical and everyday.
We were, it seems to me, like two explorers who meet quite
unexpectedly in the jungle of central Africa, greet each other

normally and in a civilised way, as if they had only the day before parted on the streets of their native town and, regarding this meeting of theirs as equally ordinary and normal, chat for a certain time about quite unimportant matters and then again, without much ceremony, disappear each in his own direction among the creepers and dark thick-leaved plants of the swamps.

Marijan, at the time of which I am speaking, was constantly wandering about the coast and islands. To me this roaming of his appeared completely senseless and purposeless, but it is very probable that to others the restless constant quests of my youth seemed the same, although they were filled with an intrinsic logic, and led by a vague star which only I was aware of.

He had discovered the forgotten house on a deserted island, and so it happened that he, I and two now already nameless girls went for a fortnight's holiday some time in the warm late spring of that forgotten year when I experienced perhaps the happiest moments of my life.

We arrived at the island in the evening and settled into the house in complete darkness—there was no electricity, nor water, nor lavatory. The house was then in a more or less respectable condition: it had two rooms and a kitchen with a huge antiquated fireplace, and when we had put together the scattered worm-eaten bits of furniture, drawing it out from under layers of dust, we succeeded in knocking together two old-fashioned double beds, a chest of drawers with no drawers, a table, and a few rickety decrepit chairs. These were the only relics of the former owners, whose identity we never established.

For some hours we clattered around the house in clouds of dust, killed scorpions, peeped into dark corners by the flickering ghostly light of wax candles. We spread patent rubber mattresses on the beds, made the entrance door usable by fixing it on to the rusty hinges, and arranged a place in a rocky spot for our night's needs, with the firm resolution that we would dig a real proper pit the next day.

So little is necessary to man for his happiness.

On the other side of the island, just that year, an old monastery was being converted into an hotel. The hotel was not yet in use, but as they had already transported things of various kinds, a watchman had settled in it, with his wife—the only people on the island besides ourselves. The watchman's wife allowed us to cook supper on her fire and in her pans. She shuddered with horror at how we could live in such a hen-house, and pitied 'such nice girls'. Her feeling of horror flattered us immeasurably. Marijan and I left the girls, of course, to busy themselves with the preparation of supper, and they went off, two bell-shaped shadows, in the silvery moonlight of the island, stumbling against gleaming rocks, enjoying their new roles, laughing a resonant, high-pitched, happy laugh which echoed in the empty heavens.

Marijan and I went round the house, like householders patting it on the walls and doorposts, and then we sat down at the table in the dark kitchen, lit two wax candles and began to play a little game of cards for two. We played for small coins, just enough for it not to be for nothing, some innocent old-age-pensioners' game, on the coarse unpainted board of the table, pelting each other with witticisms, nonsense and foolery rather than with cards, satisfied with either a loss or a win, and with ourselves. The candles flickered warmly and festively as in the olden days.

'Ho, ho, ho!' Marijan exulted. 'This is the way our ancestors lived. For the most part they saw nothing. I've again substituted an ace of hearts for an ace of diamonds.'

'It's just perfect,' I said.

'It's as good as it can be,' said Marijan.

'You've no idea about the game,' I accused him. 'Don't make excuses for yourself on account of the light.'

'With people like this I even play in the dark. If there was only a little wine for us it would be divine.'

'Where were our heads? We knew that we were going into a

wilderness. We ought to have brought drinks. A flask of wine, a book of songs and a woman, as Omar would say. We ought to have thought.'

At that moment, without knocking, without any kind of preliminary warning, with a creaking, and slowly, as if of its own accord, the door opened. It opened wide, in a dignified way, and on the doorstep, framed in darkness, flickering and ghostly from the candle-light, appeared an unearthly old man in black clothes, grey-haired and erect like the king of the spirits. He looked at us without a word, slowly, one and then the other, holding in his hands two dark bottles, not moving from the spot, a huge night bird.

We were sitting in the yellow circle of the candle-light, suddenly tiny and insignificant by contrast with the outside world, the boundless night out of which, lo! at any moment unseen ghosts might appear and bring us the unexpected. We sat, not letting out of our hands the cards, the sole contact with reality, and turning only our heads towards the solemn old man, waiting for a message from some other world, unknown and perhaps terrible. We felt as if a courier from fate itself had discovered us.

The old man contemplated us without a single word and then, with dignity, and slowly, stepped out from the vague semi-darkness in the doorway, came up to the table and placed carefully, between the candles, the two firmly corked, dark, round-bellied bottles. Once more he looked at us expressionlessly, turned rhythmically like a robot and went away, slowly and carefully closing the door behind him. At the moment when he was placing the bottles on the table I noted his eyes: they were sky-blue, empty and calm.

We sat a few more seconds motionlessly, unable to pull ourselves together, and then burst into a marvellous laugh, which did not desert us for the whole of that lovely holiday; and we opened the bottles, from which there began to gurgle out a heavy red wine, glittering and fragrant, sunny and good to drink, a wine pressed from the grapes of the stars.

We drank a few glasses solemnly, as if we were receiving the sacrament, and then a few greedily, appraising the aroma, the colour, the temperature. And soon we ceased to wonder how and whence it had come, and continued to play cards a little, to sip a little, and got drunk like Russians, by the warm candles, and began to sing, throwing cards at random on the table—to sing so heartily and so loudly that the entire old house echoed inside like a drunken barrel, suddenly again full of life, re-born.

Later the girls came with the food, and seeing us happy became happy themselves, and got drunk together with us, sang with us, in the old deserted house at the end of the world, in the small yellow circle of warm light in the midst of the vast night.

The girls explained to us that that old man was in fact the watchman of the hotel, dumb from birth, and that they had sent him, having paid for the wine. But even though paid for, happiness is still happiness.

26 From an article *His Majesty—the Newspaper Kiosk*

from the magazine *Review*

According to the writer Albert Camus, the man of today is before all else a 'devourer of newspapers'. Nor have Yugoslavs, either, managed to avoid this disease of the 20th century, expecting everything from newspapers: the truth, information, entertainment, recreation and, finally, good material for the cleaning of windows.

But on the horizon there appears the bitterest enemy of every newspaper—television! At the end of the fifties there was born in Yugoslavia a new medium, until then unknown— the journalism of motion pictures. From its appearance until today, newspapers and films have had to pass through many trials, with no brighter outlook before them. The battle becomes ever more bitter! Some newspapers founder, and those others which wish to survive are compelled to throw away their worn-out grey wardrobe and go over to colour printing. Thus are born a number of coloured illustrated papers. There are also various film magazines, which—thanks to their attractive material—have a very large number of readers. Papers which formerly had to link themselves with the cinema, describing the habits and scandals of famous stars, suddenly begin to gear themselves to television, bringing first of all information about the programme and later even the minutest intrigues and incidents from that world on the other side of the screen.

The consumer public is becoming more and more pampered. It demands that it shall be entertained, and that the newspaper shall woo it. It can no longer tolerate meagreness, a stereotyped manner of expression, a poor quality of paper and dim photography. It wishes for the best of the best, otherwise it does not appear before its newspaper kiosk at all, but with the pressure of a finger on a button opens out the spaces of the television landscape, which offers far more for far less money.

27 From an article *When the Foundations Shake*

from the magazine *Review*

The building does not stand out from others in any way. But from its foundations rhythm vibrates. It is one of those numerous Belgrade discothèques. There are more and more of them, in all the towns. And in many villages. The young people have caught on to them, and they have become a part of everyday life—those gloomy basement premises in which reigns a deafening din, where glowing lighting effects are constantly changing, when each one is alone and everyone is with everyone. In the discothèques there's no lovely old romance, couples in love, gentle melodies. The whole room shakes from sound, light and movement. The old classical dances are losing their public. To them it was necessary to go in pairs, in formal dress. Young men and girls can go alone to the discothèques, in old dungarees, remain alone and not feel lonely.

The young don't ask for much—most important are good music and the company of their contemporaries. This is the atmosphere in which they feel good and to which they like to return.

28 From the novel *The Springtimes of Ivan Galeb*

VLADAN DESNICA

Today the sky at dawn was overcast. Only in mid-morning did the sun appear and lure me like a lizard to the window. I interrupted my writing and stood behind the window pane looking at the narrow space with cultivated borders between the two pavilions. Suddenly a motor-car roared up and stopped before the entrance to the building. The black, shiny, rounded roof gleamed in the sunshine. Out of the motor-car there tumbled an entire little family: father, mother, daughter—already a grown girl—and a little son. Without doubt they had come on a visit to someone. The father slammed the rear door, not omitting, before that, to let the window down a little for the sake of ventilation, so that it would not be stuffy later. Then he drew out of his pocket a little clinking bunch of small keys, and with a tiny flat brass Yale carefully locked up. For the door in front he did not show a similar fatherly care; this he only slammed. They passed up the staircase, slightly more noisily than pedestrian visitors, and then their steps were heard in the corridor right until they disappeared into my neighbour's room. The door which closed behind them cut off from my ear the voices raised in surprise and greeting on meeting.

The boy remained only a brief while in the room. I imagine that even during that space of time he was shifting from one foot to the other, and counting silently up to one hundred, or three hundred, or whatever he had already decided in advance was the least time that he need stay with the invalid. And then he stole out and went down again to his friend the motor-car. Obviously a quite recent acquisition. He drew out from beneath the front seat a large new duster of chamois leather, and began to wipe the glass, the shining metal of the radiator, the head-lamps. Then he sat down at the steering wheel (I saw him diagonally, through the window which had been wiped, beneath the low roof), and began, in turn, to press with his feet on the controls, lightly to turn the steering wheel this way and that, 'on dry land', as it were. At the same time he pursed his lips; he was completing the illusion, imitating the sound of the motor. Then he set into motion the windscreen wiper, which turned right-left, right-left, straining slightly over the dry glass, for today, you see, unfortunately there isn't a drop of rain. Really, children are unlucky! There never happens to be for them what there ought to be at that moment!

And upstairs, meanwhile, in the room, they were chattering and prattling. They were asking the invalid questions about himself, about his health, not giving him time to answer but cutting into his answers, just begun, with new questions, breaking into one another's remarks, and shouting each other down . . . In their chatter, without doubt, at least ten times there recurred the words 'car', 'our car', in various cases, as in exercises in declensions. They had seen that it was a fine day and had thought: why don't we take advantage of it and pop off in our car to visit him? It's true, the road isn't extremely good, but the car is new, it has good springs, and never mind, we'll drive rather more slowly. And so they had taken their seats in the car, Victor had sat down at the steering wheel and lit a cigarette, and the cigarette had not yet burned to the end and already they were there . . . But where's Zvonko? He always sneaks off somewhere! Oh, he's surely down below, with the car . . . Only, for heaven's sake, as long as he doesn't touch anything! . . . But he won't, he won't, no need to worry, he's sensible about these things . . . Good Lord, it's to be understood, it interests him a lot; after all, he's a child, we've all been children . . . And here their faces, delighted, turn collectively to the invalid for confirmation and under-standing.

But now they really must go, they've stayed a long time. Victor in fact has one more little job to do before luncheon, only they don't know—does the invalid know, perhaps?—no, unfortunately the invalid does not know—wouldn't it be better for them on the way back to go by the upper road? Why should they return by the same road when they can . . . but no, no, there's no sense in that, the upper road is somewhat shorter, to be sure, but why run the risk, for like this, with our car, it means only a few minutes' difference, and that's nothing, there really is no sense in wearing the car out. Anyway, the lower road, however, by which they had come, was on the whole quite decent, and why should they now risk . . . but they really were glad that the invalid looked so well, honestly, really well, they were delighted, and they hoped that soon, quite soon, and so on . . . Well then, once more, they're glad, they're delighted, with all their hearts, they're delighted, they stand up, button up their overcoats, check travelling coats of tweed, and hope that he'll soon, quite soon . . . Oh, Lord! They had quite forgotten they'd brought flowers, a few gladioli, beautiful fresh gladioli, they had leaned them there against the radiator . . . Oh, thank you, thank you . . . and they hope that he'll soon, quite soon . . . thank you . . . well then, au revoir, see you again soon, thank you, thank you, once again, au revoir!—and finally they depart.

They pass along the corridor again, go down the stairs, graciously smile at the doorman. Victor extracts from his pocket the little clinking shining bunch, selects the tiny flat brass key, carefully inserts it in the little lock, unlocks the little rear door, lets the window down a little lower still. But Zvonko really hadn't behaved nicely, what would the invalid say, what sort of opinion of him would he have? But really it's a lovely day, and it's good that they had taken advantage of it, because one doesn't know about tomorrow yet, one never knows quite for certain about tomorrow! . . . And luckily there's not much dust. And the invalid really hadn't made such a bad impression on her. Nor on him, nor on him, he had expected a worse, much worse one. They settle themselves in the car. Victor sits down at the steering wheel, lights another cigarette, adjusts his little hat, the little green hat with the edelweiss, and draws a last leg into the car. Zvonko sits down beside him. The slammed doors give little pleuritic coughs—and the car starts.

From the novel *The Cyclops*

RANKO MARINKOVIĆ

High up on the roof of a palatial building MAAR-ADVERTISING-CENTRE unfolded a canvas when darkness had fallen, and began to shout. When he has written out over the canvas, with a mysterious light, his powerful name, MAAR's letters perform a crazy little show, singing in unison some song in honour of their master. Then they skip away into the darkened sky, and he once more shouts to the awestruck people: MAAR SOUND-FILM ADVERTISING.

There then appears a house, wretched and dirty, its roof aslant, its door collapsed, and from its windows in panic terror there jump out crumpled and messy shirts, ghostly torsos without head and legs. To the music of the Danse Macabre the sick victims of uncleanliness drag themselves towards a boiler upon a fire, in which a dense white lather is bubbling impatiently. With old-maidish distrust, hesitating still on the very edge of the boiler (they are afraid lest they trick them), the shirts jump into the lather . . . and lo! the distrust was the result of stupid prejudice, for see how one after another, dazzling white, they come out of the boiler and, marching in a line, sing enthusiastically: 'Radion washes alone.' Then on the canvas a sphinx has appeared, and asks the spectators in a far-away voice as from the desert: 'Is this possible?' And immediately a lovely shorthand-typist demonstrates how it is not possible to write on two machines simultaneously. 'And is this possible?' asks the sphinx. No, that is not possible either—for water to flow uphill. And neither is this possible, for a house to be built from the roof, nor for the sun to revolve around the earth . . .'But it *is* possible that "Tungsram Crypton" lamps, with twice coiled filament, give doubly strong light for the same expenditure of current.' . . . and there shone out on the canvas a lamp like the heavenly sun, so that it was even necessary to blink from the frightful glare. Then on to the canvas comes dancing a frisky little girl in a spotted dirndl frock and recites in the innocent-little-girl's voice of a boarder at the Reverend Sisters': 'Zora soap washes marvellously, really one must admit —admit, one must',* she corrects her mistake, to no purpose; the spectators laugh. The little girl withdraws, abashed. After the little girl there follows a traveller; he drags two heavy trunks, and behind him winds a highroad in endless perspective. The sun, from above, beats the traveller with fiery whips, but he strides lightly and merrily, and winking slily he whispers to the audience in confidence: 'With "Palma" heels you traverse a long road without any fatigue at all' and he displays enormous soles: yes, it's true, 'Palma' heels! . . . Kastner and Öhler, the largest department store in the Balkans, has poured from its horn of plenty unbelievable and marvellous things, 'from a needle to a lorry', and the imagination of the spectators pecks, pecks among these luxuries. Julijo Meini wants to satisfy everybody's thirst with Chinese, Ceylon and even Russian tea, and of the coffees only 'Hag' coffee, because it spares your heart. Sneeze if you can after Bayer's aspirin! While you sleep, 'Darmol' works, and 'Planinka' tea has the patriotic duty of cleansing Aryan blood. 'Elida' cream trembles for your complexion. 'Interkozma' vows that it will, in the shortest time, afforest your denuded head. 'Kalodont' is the bitter enemy of dental tartar, and V-H-G asks you roguishly if you are a man. And at the end, 'The first Croatian establishment for fine funerals', with the greatest respect, takes the liberty of reminding you of your dignity and . . . be so good as to look: a black lacquered carriage with gold baroque angels, horses with shining black hair, a comfortable coffin, an escort of ideally sober personnel with admirals' hats, and thus your death is yet one more success and a thing of beauty, quite poetic. . . .

* *She has lost the rhyme in Serbo-Croat by reversing the word order.*

Part III

NOTES AND BIBLIOGRAPHY

Notes

Those readers who have studied Serbo-Croat from a Grammar in which most attention has been given to the *e*-dialect (such as *Teach Yourself Serbo-Croat*), and have so far had little experience of the *ije*-dialect, will notice certain characteristics of this dialect in the passages by Croatian writers and in the extract from the short story by Ivo Andrić, who formerly wrote in this dialect. Those occurring most frequently are the ending *-io* where the *e*-dialect has *-eo* (*dio; htio, vidio, volio*); the forms of the pronouns *nitko* and *tko*; the use of *što* as the interrogative 'what?'; frequent use of the indefinite endings in the declension of adjectives; future tense forms such as *imat će*; and a tendency to place an enclitic auxiliary verb, and the reflexive pronoun *se*, very near to the beginning of a sentence. The extract from the novel by Mihailo Lalić illustrates characteristics of the *ije*-dialect as spoken in Montenegro.

Many tenses will be found in the narrative passages in this book where English would only use a past tense. Serbo-Croat uses not only the compound past tense, the pluperfect, the aorist and the imperfect, but also very frequently the historic present. (You will also come across a historic future.) The historic present must be recognised, but in the translations a past tense has usually been substituted for it.

The Latin alphabet has been used throughout this book as it makes for easier reading, being naturally more familiar than Cyrillic to English-speaking students. In Yugoslavia many books, including some represented here (e.g. those by Ivo Andrić and Mihailo Lalić), are published in editions in each alphabet.

The following abbreviations have been used in the notes:

acc. (accusative)

adj. (adjective)

adv. (adverb)

dat. (dative)

fem. (feminine)

fn. (footnote)

gen. (genitive)

infin. (infinitive)

instr. (instrumental)

ipf. (imperfective)

lit. (literally)

masc. (masculine)

neut. (neuter)

nom. (nominative)

pers. (person)

pf. (perfective)

pl. (plural)

pres. (present)

sing. (singular)

TYS-Cr (*Teach Yourself Serbo-Croat*. See Bibliography.)

The publication dates given in these Notes are those of the first editions. The dates of the editions used in this book are given in the Bibliography.

p. 13 DRAGUTIN TADIJANOVIĆ (b. 1905), a Croat, is best known as a lyric poet. The items given here are from a small collection of his autobiographical prose works contained in Pjesme i proza (1969).

STRAH U ŽELJEZNICI

u svibnju: 'in May'. TYS-Cr p. 90.

. . . *sam se vozio:* 'I was driven' (lit. 'I drove myself'). TYS-Cr p. 79.

mati: TYS-Cr p. 139.

ocu: dat. sing.; TYS-Cr p. 112.

mjeseci: gen. pl.; TYS-Cr p. 139.

purš (German *Bursch*), *posilni:* both are nouns, and their meanings are similar.

sobom: the preposition *sa* is often omitted before the reflexive pronoun in the instrumental case.

kao da: 'it is' or 'it was' are often to be understood before this expression, 'it's as if', 'it's as though, 'it was as if', etc.

dolaska: nom. *dolazak;* TYS-Cr pp. 29 and 111.

dob: fem., declined like *stvar* (TYS-Cr p. 30); not to be confused with *doba* (TYS-Cr p. 141).

jače: 'rather strongly'. This use of the comparative form of adjectives and adverbs is common.

razvijen: TYS-Cr p. 130. See also *savijenim* (p. 22 this Reader).

bojale su se da će morati: reported speech. TYS-Cr p. 65 and p. 39, fn. 1.

čitavu kartu: acc. after *platiti:* 'to pay for'.

djecu: TYS-Cr p. 140.

u ruci: TYS-Cr p. 45.

što više: TYS-Cr p. 98.

ramena: nom. sing. *rame*; TYS-Cr p. 20 (see *ime*).

kako ne bi imao: lit. 'how would he not have'.

p. 14 *on će majci:* this use of *će*, to mean '[he or she] said', is not unusual in narrative.

Dajte vaše karte: colloquially, or for the sake of emphasis, other possessive adjectives are often used when *svoj*, the reflexive possessive adjective, might be expected. Note that in the first sentence of this narrative, and elsewhere in it, *svoj* has been used. TYS-Cr p. 45.

junače: nom. *junak*; 'hero'.

nek te voda nosi: lit. 'let the water bear you [along]'.

da i on čuje: lit. 'that he too hears'.

neće . . . ništa: an infinitive is understood.

p. 15 NAS TROJE

This is the middle section of a short prose narrative. The boy had already talked with the poet and gone; later there comes a woman, the third member of the 'trio'.

troje: TYS-Cr p. 141.

u moju blizinu: lit. 'to my vicinity'.

Vojnovićeva: TYS-Cr p. 45.

notes: French *notes*. 2 syllables.

prekriživši nogu preko noge: lit. 'having crossed leg across leg'.

dvojicom: TYS-Cr p. 142.

pročitaj mu ime: mu is a possessive dative. TYS-Cr p. 151.

polaziti školu: 'to attend school'. Another verb must be supplied in English with *nauke* ('studies') as its object.

p. 16 *poginuti:* 'to perish'; here, as usually, 'to be killed'.

tjemenu: nom. sing. *tjeme;* TYS-Cr p. 20 (see *ime*).

p. 17 ŠIMO ŠIMIĆ

This is another extract from a prose narrative.

Šimi: first names ending -o, even though denoting males, are sometimes declined as fem. nouns.

kolima: nom. *kola;* always neut. pl; TYS-Cr p. 141.

dočekati: 'to wait until the expected person arrives', hence sometimes 'to meet' (e.g. at a station), and hence the translation 'to wait up' in this context.

prozebao: infin. *prozepsti;* active past participle with adjectival use. TYS-Cr p. 34 fn.

ko ti je taj?: ti is an ethic dative. TYS-Cr p. 151.

ovo je bijeda: TYS-Cr p. 44.

kako li bi me bilo strah: TYS-Cr p. 152.

p. 18 *u mrklome mraku:* lit. 'in gloomy darkness.'

obučen u . . . odijelo: note the acc., 'dressed into . . . clothes'.

obuven u (obuti, obujem): 'shod in' (again with acc.).

opanak: a flat leather shoe, worn by peasants.

obojica: TYS-Cr p. 143.

. . . mene i nema: lit. 'there isn't of me'. TYS-Cr p. 136.

Čuj me!: lit. 'Hear me!'

već kako koji dan: an expression which cannot be translated literally. It suggests that each day she gave him whichever was to be had of such things.

p. 19 *očima:* TYS-Cr p. 125.

kakó bi se domogao: domoći se, domognem se, with gen.; 'to reach, get as far as'.

granulo je: 'burst forth'.

Marića brdo: 'the hill of the Marić family'.

da ga doziva: lit. 'that [it] keeps calling him'.

uteko: a contraction of *utekao* (*uteći, utečem*).

p. 20 The *Narodne pripovijetke* ('Folk Tales') from which the next item was taken were compiled by TVRTKO ČUBELIĆ of Zagreb University, who has compiled and edited many anthologies and collections of folk tales.

LAV I ČOVJEK

grudi: fem. pl.; TYS-Cr p. 140.

mira: partitive gen.; TYS-Cr pp. 136, 150.

za čim (instr.) *je pošao:* lit. 'after which he had set out'.

obraslu: lit. 'overgrown'. TYS-Cr p. 34, fn.

p. 21 *uzjaše:* infinitive *uzjahati.*

upravljati: with instr.; TYS-Cr p. 180.

zemlja se kao potresla: lit. 'the earth [was] as [if] it shook'.

odskače: infinitive *odskakati.*

ržući: infinitive *rzati.*

sluga: fem. in form, masc. in meaning. TYS-Cr p. 139.

u čovjeka: TYS-Cr p. 184.

Što bi s njime?: lit. 'What would [you] with him?'

braći: TYS-Cr p. 139.

neka: TYS-Cr p. 124.

po snazi: nom. *snaga;* lit. 'according to strength'.

jača od najjačih sila: lit. 'stronger than the strongest forces'.

p. 22 The following four items and nos. 19, 20, 21, 22, 26 and 27 are adapted extracts from articles in *Revija* ('Review'), an illustrated magazine concerned entirely with Yugoslavia and Yugoslav affairs, published in Belgrade but issued in various languages, including English.

I TREBNJE JE ROĐENO

stotinu: TYS-Cr p. 90, fn. 2.

centar okupljanja: lit. 'centre of rallying'.

među sobom: lit. 'among themselves'.

jedni za druge: lit. 'the ones about the others'.

građani: sing. *građanin*; TYS-Cr p. 125.

drvetu: nom. *drvo*; TYS-Cr p. 20.

postavljeni, formirana: TYS-Cr p. 128, 'The past tense is often implicit in the [passive] participle itself.' See also the title of this item.

p. 23 PLANINSKI TURIZAM

Note how the object of the first sentence has preceded the subject. TYS-Cr p. 70.

hiljadu: TYS-Cr p. 90, fn. 2.

nazvali „zemljom . . .": TYS-Cr p. 180.

kontinentalni deo: lit. 'continental part'.

uticalo je da . . . : lit. 'has influenced that . . .'.

sve više: TYS-Cr p. 98.

p. 24 PAKAO U DOLINI RAJA

ugnezdilo se seoce: lit. 'the hamlet has nestled'.

pred jednu . . . pećinu; pred pećinom: TYS-Cr, p. 184.

p. 25 DUGO PUTOVANJE SEDOG PESNIKA

VLADIMIR NAZOR, 1876–1949, and IVAN GORAN KOVAČIĆ, 1913–43, who was killed in the war, were two of the greatest 20th century Croatian poets.

u . . . petoj ofanzivi: 'in the 5th [enemy] offensive'.

prihvatio pušku: lit. 'took up a gun'.

korpu jagoda: they would have been wild strawberries.

da im oprosti grehe: lit. 'that he forgive sins to them'. TYS-Cr p. 179.

Vlade, Vladu: see note p. 173, on the name 'Šimo'. The form Nazora is acc. sing. of masc. 'animate' noun.

što se mene tiče: TYS-Cr p. 178.

oče: TYS-Cr p. 110.

pokaza rukom: lit. 'showed (indicated) with his hand'.

p. 26 ANTONIJE ISAKOVIĆ (b. 1923) is a Serbian writer of short stories , of which *Veče*, although it comes from his earliest collection *Velika deca* (1953), is in many respects characteristic, illustrating as it does the writer's sympathy with the sufferings of simple people in the midst of war, and his consciousness of the futility of the waste and misery caused by it. Three extracts from *Veče* are given here.

The narrator, after fighting with the Partisans, has been appointed a staff officer at headquarters in a remote part of south-west Bosnia. He is resting on the doorstep of a *bačija*, a mountain herdsman's hut and dairy.

VEČE

ćebad: fem. sing. collective noun. TYS-Cr p. 181. *ćebetu*, nom. *ćebe*. TYS-Cr p. 20.

tanja: TYS-Cr p. 97.

s tobom da pričamo: lit. 'to tell [about things] with you'. Bosnian peasants freely address a stranger as *ti*.

stri... čeva: TYS-Cr p. 110.

p. 27 *strigao (strići, strižem):* lit. 'to shear'.

kamenje: neut. sing. collective noun. TYS-Cr pp. 140–1.

pasti na pamet: lit. 'to fall on to one's mind'.

podigoh ramena: 'to shrug the shoulders' is *sleći* or *slegnuti* (pf.), *slegati* (ipf.) *ramenima.* TYS-G p. 181.

p. 28 *Čitavu šumu izgorimo, kako neće?:* lit. 'We're burning up the whole forest, how won't it?', i.e. 'how can it possibly not end?'

Nemamo braće: brat, pl. *braća:* TYS-Cr p. 139. Gen. *braće* after *nemamo,* 'we haven't any brothers'.

devojke: 'young girls', 'grown girls', older than *devojčice.*

Srbijanac: a Serb whose ancestors and family have remained in Serbia.

p. 29 *Šipad:* a Bosnian timber firm.

Glamočko Polje: a region in Bosnia.

učiti školu: lit. 'to study school' (the usual expression).

tek oko ponoći: only about midnight, not earlier.

Dobila si ga?: dobiti can mean 'to get', 'to gain', 'to earn', 'to be given'.

p. 30 *Osećao sam . . . dlanove kako počinju:* TYS-Cr p. 146.

Pije mi se voda: it is not uncommon to use *piti* as a reflexive verb in this sense.

p. 31 *gromuljica:* lit. 'a tiny lump' of any substance.

p. 32 *ostane:* infin. *ostati;* this verb, 'to remain', often corresponds to 'to be left'.

leđa: 'back' (of body); neut. pl.; TYS-Cr p. 141.

p. 33 IVAN SLAMNIG (b. 1930), is a Croatian poet, prose writer and translator. The extract given here is the first part of a short story in the form of a monologue. The refrain which occurs twice in this passage is repeated a third time, ending the work.

MOJ SIN

imam mnogo toga misliti: a construction in normal colloquial usage, but which cannot be explained grammatically. ('To think about'—*misliti o*, with loc.)

smokinzima: TYS-Cr p. 108.

konzervi: gen. pl.; nom. *konzerva*.

odabranica: lit. 'chosen girl or woman'.

nije me briga: briga me je is a similar construction to *strah me je*, TYS-Cr p. 152.

p. 34 *mislim njegovu situaciju u Južnoj Americi:* i.e. 'I mean the situation if he is in South America.'

što nije baš u redu: lit. 'which is not quite in order'.

pukotina: lit. 'crack'.

u . . . lovovima: lit. 'in . . . hunts'.

radi se o: 'it's a matter of, a question of'.

što se ne javlja: javljati se (pf. *javiti se*) may mean to write, telephone, call or communicate in any way, according to the context; also to present oneself, announce oneself.

humak: lit. 'mound'. *Grob* is the usual word for 'grave'.

p. 35 *da je švercovao:* an 'unreal' condition. TYS-Cr p. 119.

cijev: lit. 'pipe', 'tube'.

djelovati: 'to have an effect', 'to operate'.

svježe: 'freshly' (adv.).

šareniti se: to make an impression of colours and patterns. The adjective *šaren* means 'variegated' 'patterned'.

p. 36 *četnici:* followers of Mihajlović in World War II.

    ustaše: Croatian quislings.

    ni od koga: TYS-Cr p. 103.

    prebjegavanje: lit. 'fleeing across'.

p. 37 RADOMIR KONSTANTINOVIĆ (b.1928) is a Serbian novelist whose works are characterised by their originality and psychological penetration. His novel *Daj nam danas* was first published in 1954.

    The speaker, Anna, is recalling the day of her marriage.

DAJ NAM DANAS

    ljudi: gen. pl.; TYS-Cr p. 139.

    odmahivao glavom: TYS-Cr p. 180 (*mahnuti*).

p. 38 *ostaci:* TYS-Cr pp. 111–12.

p. 39 *nije sve bilo u tome:* lit. 'not all was in that'.

    fotograf, fotografija: note that these mean 'photographer' and 'photograph' respectively.

    cveće: neut. sing. collective. TYS-Cr pp. 140–1.

p. 40 *napregnute pažnje:* genitive of description. TYS-Cr p. 150.

    Mogli smo da igramo: 'we could dance' or 'we could have danced', according to the context. (Here the latter.) TYS-Cr p. 116.

p. 41 IVO ANDRIĆ (b. 1892), prominent Serbian novelist and short story writer, was awarded the Nobel prize for literature in 1961. Much of his work has been translated into English.

ČUDO U OLOVU, which is in many respects characteristic of Andrić's novels and short stories, tells of the unhappy married life of the wife of the wealthy and debauched

Bademlić. (His 'sensual smile' is recalled, significantly, towards the end of the present extract.) All their children had died while young except the last one, a mentally and physically helpless little girl, whom the mother is now taking to the Spring of Our Lady in the hope of a cure. The extract given here ends with the 'miracle', but the story goes on to an unexpected development, and the actual end is deeply moving.

Andrić's later works are in the *e*-dialect, but this early work (1931) is in the *ije*-dialect. The extract is taken from a 1958 collection of his stories.

granje: neut. sing. collective. TYS-Cr pp. 140–1.

smiješila se . . . smiješkom: instr.; TYS-Cr p. 181 (see *živeti . . . životom,* etc.).

očima: instr. pl.

Bademlićka: a feminine form of the husband's name.

molila . . . krunicu: lit. 'prayed the rosary'.

iram, dimije: loan words from Turkish.

majčin: TYS-Cr p. 110.

odmahnuo glavom: TYS-Cr p. 181.

p. 42 *momci:* sing. *momak.*

Gospina vrela: Gospodičina vrela.

Bademlićevi: surnames ending -*ić* take this plural ending.

vatara: gen. pl.; TYS-Cr p. 29.

ostavljane: the passive participle of the imperfective verb, 'were being left'.

p. 43 *uši:* TYS-Cr p. 125.

mišlju, instr. sing. of *misao,* fem.: TYS-Cr pp. 30 and 112.

zaova joj: possessive dative. TYS-Cr p. 151.

podbratka: nom. *podbradak;* TYS-Cr p. 111.

p. 45 PETAR ŠEGEDIN (b. 1909), a Croat, is a writer in many fields. His perceptive observation of humanity, a characteristic of his work, is illustrated in the extract given here from *Na putu* (1953), an account of the writer's thoughts and experiences during his travels.

NA PUTU

karta: this word may be used with the meaning 'menu', but *jelovnik* is more usual.

nek (neka) mu se donese: TYS-Cr p. 124.

i dalje: TYS-Cr p. 98.

držao sam se pasivno: lit. 'I behaved (held myself) passively'.

ocrtavati: lit. 'to delineate'.

s v o j i m : note that words are emphasised in print by spacing in this way, where in English italic characters would be used.

p. 46 *savršenost:* lit. 'perfection', 'completeness', 'precision'.

slobodan prostor: lit. 'free space'.

p. 47 MIHAILO LALIĆ (b. 1914), a native of Montenegro, is a writer of novels and short stories with the horrors of the war years as their principal theme. The pages given here from the novel *Zlo proljeće* (1953) represent a nostalgic interlude.

ZLO PROLJEĆE

nalaziti se: lit. 'to find oneself', 'to be situated'.

žbunje, drveće, lišće: neut. sing. collective nouns. TYS-Cr pp. 140–1.

nijesu: the Montenegrin form.

p. 48 *kad propadaše mnogo stoke:* The cattle (*stoka*, fem. sing.) were perishing in a great drought.

prelazi: lit. 'crosses over', 'passes over'.

doviđenja (or *do viđenja*): means literally 'au revoir', and therefore has not that sound of finality which 'goodbye' may have.

p. 49 *pozaboravljao:* the prefix *po* here gives a frequentative sense to the imperfective verb *zaboravljati*.

(*ako neće biti*) *novog viđenja:* lit. 'any new seeing' (partitive gen.).

p. 50 MEŠA SELIMOVIĆ (b. 1910), a Bosnian, achieved prominence with the publication of his novel *Derviš i smrt* (1966), but was already well known for his earlier works. The extract given here from *Tišine* (1965) illustrates the dominant theme of the novel, which contains a variety of episodes and well-drawn characters. It is set in Zagreb.

TIŠINE

ma šta: TYS-Cr p. 146.

krš: lit. 'rocky, barren land'.

molim: lit. 'I beg', 'I pray', hence 'please'; but as used here it is simply a curt response.

p. 51 *pričam o lasici:* the narrator has visited his pre-war girl friend, to whom he had given the nickname *lasica* ('weasel').

ispovijedanje: lit. 'the making of confessions'.

mišica: 'upper arm'.

p. 52 *struka:* 'profession', 'line', 'métier'.

sakato: lit. 'crippled'.

Duško se smijao mojoj priči: TYS-Cr p. 180 (see *smejati se*).

p. 53 *nisam zamjerao svom . . . položaju:* TYS-Cr p. 180 (see *zameriti*).

ma kakvo: TYS-Cr p. 146.

vrlo važno: used similarly in an ironic sense in the extract from Slobodan Novak (p. 64).

p. 55 NIKOLA ŠOP (b. 1904), a Croatian poet whose work has been translated into English by W. H. Auden and B. Brusar, is also a writer in other fields. The three items given here, together with others on the same theme, are included in a volume of his short prose works, *Tajanstvena prela* (1943).

KASNI POSJETILAC

gušenje: lit. 'muffling'.

svlačenje kaputa: lit. 'the drawing off of a coat'.

dugmad: fem. sing. collective noun. There is also a regular plural form. TYS-Cr pp. 20 and 181.

njega još nema: TYS-Cr p. 136.

Odluka je pala: lit. 'the decision has fallen'.

nitko: lit. 'nobody'.

gostiju: gen. pl. The form *gosti* is also in use.

p. 56 GOST STRAŠILO

strašilo: a noun, in apposition to *gost,* and meaning a scarecrow, or any terrifying creature.

bojati se: TYS-Cr p. 178.

nego: 'but', with the sense of 'on the other hand'.

obaspu: infin. *obasuti.*

što laskavijim: TYS-Cr p. 98.

p. 57 RASTRESENI GOST

u kome je vodio prvu riječ: lit. 'in which he was leading the first word'. *Riječ* (which is understood) is the subject of the following clause.

zape: aorist; infin. *zapeti,* pres. *zapne.*

srkati: pres. *srčem;* 'to sip'.

oprostiti se sa: 'to take leave of'.

načuditi se (with dat.): TYS-Cr p. 178 (*čuditi se*).

pojam: gen. *pojma;* 'idea', 'inkling'. *Nemam ni pojma,* 'I've no idea'.

For a note on the following four items see p. 173.

Grad slavne prošlosti
sati: gen. pl.; TYS-Cr p. 139.

p. 60 Novembar u Beogradu

stotine: gen. sing., 'of a hundred'; *hiljada,* gen. pl. TYS-Cr p. 86.

Beograđana: TYS-Cr p. 125.

vrtići: lit. 'little gardens'.

centri zdravstvene zaštite: lit. 'centres of health protection'.

stambeni četvrti: lit. 'residential quarters'.

nikao: infin. *nići* or *niknuti,* pres. *niknem* (pf.), 'to spring up' (of plants). Used figuratively here.

udarile su: lit. 'struck'.

objekt: in this context this noun has a wide though special meaning, covering buildings and institutions with various practical purposes.

niču: infin. *nicati* (ipf.). See *nići,* above.

p. 61 Titograd

na dvanaestom kilometru: lit. 'at the 12th kilometre'.

potiče: infin. *poticati,* lit. 'originates'.

iz IV veka pre naše ere: lit. 'from the 4th century before our era'.

niz: lit. 'series', 'row'. This noun is used very freely, followed by a gen. pl. and often preceded by *ceo*, 'a whole', to mean 'a large number'.

umetnički: lit. 'artistic'.

p. 62 PRUGA BEOGRAD-BAR

spada u: lit. 'falls into'.

da bi . . . isplovila: lit. 'that it may sail out'.

svega: 'in all'.

nadmorske visine: lit. 'of above-sea height'.

legu: infin. *leći*, pres. *ležem* etc., but 3rd pers. pl. *legu.*

p. 63 SLOBODAN NOVAK (b. 1924) is a writer from the Adriatic Coast, a poet and novelist. The narrator in his novel *Mirisi zlato i tamjan* (1957) relates with much candour his experiences while his wife is away and he is left alone in charge of an aged bed-ridden woman, Madona, in her house on an island off the Adriatic coast. His wife is now returning.

MIRISI, ZLATO I TAMJAN

tušta i tma (with gen. pl.): an idiomatic, colloquial expression.

tri tovara blaga: quoted from a well-known folk poem.

nešto izvodim bez veze: lit. 'I'm doing something with no connection'.

usran: 'bloody' is quite a mild translation.

smak svijeta: smak is used only in this phrase.

zašto ne, izvolite, samo ubijte! A colloquial, ironical expression of annoyance, lit. 'Why don't you, please, just kill?', i.e. 'Just go ahead and kill me, please, why not?'

p. 64 *nije . . . dala:* 'refused'.

vrlo važno: this expression was used ironically also towards the end of the extract from Selimović's *Tišine*.

p. 65 *smireno:* adverb from passive participle (*smiren*, 'calmed').

p. 66 ALEKSANDAR VUČO (b. 1897) is a Serbian novelist. His novel *Raspust* (1954), from which an extract is given here, has been translated into English (see Bibliography). It concerns the experiences and memories of its central character Dragan, in World War I.

RASPUST

užina: a more suitable translation would have been 'tea' if chocolate had not been the drink served. It is any light meal between the principal meals.

četvoro: TYS-Cr p. 141.

sreće: infin. *sretati.*

skandirajući reči: lit. 'scanning the words'.

p. 67 *Ko bi rekao!:* lit. 'Who would have said!'

sirće: declined like *dugme.* TYS-Cr p. 20.

snovi: sing. *san.* TYS-Cr p. 113.

udati se za (with acc.): 'to marry' (of a woman).

očev: TYS-Cr p. 110.

p. 68 *u osice:* TYS-Cr p. 184.

bujati: lit. 'to be luxuriant', 'grow luxuriantly'.

to ste vi: TYS-Cr p. 44.

p. 69 *a da ne zadrhtim:* lit. 'but that I do not begin to tremble'. *Zadrhtati* is a perfective verb, suggesting a sudden fit of trembling.

zavladati (with instr.): TYS-Cr p. 180 (see *vladati*).

Da sam ja slušala: 'unreal' condition. TYS-Cr p. 119.

p. 70 ANTUN ŠOLJAN (b. 1932), a Croat, is a prose writer in
many fields and a poet. The passage given here is an
extract from a short story, one of a sequence published
under the title *Izdajice* (1961).

ROĐENDAN

poštovanja: gen., 'any respect'. TYS-Cr p. 150.

Ljubavnice: girl friends, mistresses.

u njima je uvijek bilo neke težine: gen., 'in them was
always something of significance', lit. 'some weightiness'.

prirodno, logično, svakodnevno: adverbs, but translated as
adjectives.

p. 71 *smatrajući . . . običnim:* instr.; TYS-Cr p. 153.

među lijane: lit. 'to among the creepers'. TYS-Cr p. 183.

lišće: 'foliage', and (below) *posuđe:* 'pots and pans', neut.
sing. collective nouns. TYS-Cr pp. 140–1.

bračan: lit. 'conjugal', 'marital'.

p. 72 *i sami sobom:* lit. 'and ourselves with ourselves'.

preci: nom. sing. *predak.* TYS-Cr pp. 111–12.

Da nam je još samo malo vina: 'unreal' condition. TYS-Cr
p. 119.

p. 73 *ruku:* gen. pl.; TYS-Cr p. 140.

zatvorivši: lit. 'having closed'. TYS-Cr pp. 145–6.

crveno vino: lighter in colour than dark red wine, which
is called *crno vino*, 'black wine'. *Iskričavo* has been translated 'glittering' rather than 'sparkling', because 'sparkling' (of wine) is *p(j)enušavo*.

kao pijana bačva: a colloquial simile.

p. 75 For a note on the following two items see p. 173.

NJEGOVO VELIČANSTVO—KIOSK ZA NOVINE

sve ogorčenija: 'ever more embittered; (and below) *sve razmaženija*, 'ever more spoiled'. TYS-Cr p. 98.

rađa se: lit. 'is born', but the past tense is to be understood.

propadaju: infin. *propadati*, ipf., lit. 'to be failing', 'going bankrupt'.

na obojene tiraže: lit. 'to coloured *tirages*.'

da se vezuju: lit. 'that they link (bind, connect) themselves'.

s one strane: 'on the far side'.

bledu (fotografiju): lit. 'pale'.

p. 76 KADA SE TEMELJI TRESU

ničim ne: lit. 'by nothing'. TYS-Cr p. 102.

sve . . . više: TYS-Cr p. 98.

u mnogim selima: 'many', more usually the adverb *mnogo* (with gen.), is here an adjective, agreeing with *selima*.

u koju se rado vraćaju: lit. 'to which they gladly return'.

p. 77 VLADAN DESNICA (1905–67), a Croat, is the only writer represented in this book who is not alive as this book goes to press. In his novel *Proljeća Ivana Galeba* (1957), from which an extract is given here, accounts of the narrator's experiences alternate with his observations and reminiscences as he lies in hospital.

PROLJEĆA IVANA GALEBA

doći u pohode: although *pohode* is plural, this expression means 'to come on a visit'.

stotinu: TYS-Cr p. 90, fn. 2.

p. 78 *ni za lijek:* an idiomatic expression, frequently used; lit. 'not even for [a drop of] medicine'.

ne davali vremena: the auxiliary verb is omitted; *vremena,* a partitive gen.; TYS-Cr p. 150.

upadali u: lit. 'fell into'.

jedno drugom: lit. 'one to another'.

našim kolima: for *svojim kolima.* See note above, under Tadijanović, *Strah u željeznici (Dajte vaše karte),* p. 170.

na koncu konca: lit. 'at the end of the end *(konac)'.*

razdragana lica: gen. of description. TYS-Cr p. 150.

nema smisla: 'there's no sense' (gen.). For the declension of *smisao* (masc.) see TYS-Cr p. 112, *posao.*

baš im je drago: 'they really are glad'. *Drago mi je* and *milo mi je* (lit. 'it is dear to me') are commonly used for 'I am glad'.

itakodalje: i tako dalje. TYS-Cr p. 98.

p. 80 RANKO MARINKOVIĆ (b. 1913) is a Croatian novelist and short story writer. The passage from his novel *Kiklop* (1966) which is given here occurs also in one of his short stories.

KIKLOP

platno: lit. 'canvas', but could be translated more freely as 'screen' here.

odskakuću: 'they skip away'; infin. *odskakutati.*

iskaču: 'they jump out'; infin. *iskakati.*

nogu: gen. pl.; TYS-Cr p. 140.

kotlu: nom. *kotao;* see the declension of *posao,* TYS-Cr p. 112.

gledaoce: nom. sing. *gledalac;* TYS-Cr p. 113 (see declension of *čitalac).*

teče: 'flows' (infin. *teći).*

okreće se: 'turns', 'revolves' (infin. *okretati se*).

nit: fem., declined like *stvar*; 'twice coiled filament', i.e. 'coiled coil'.

p. 81 ... *mora priznat* ... *priznat mora:* the word order is grammatically correct in both versions.

putnika: acc. sing.; the object of *bije*.

potpetica: heel of a boot or shoe; the heel of a foot is *peta*.

iz roga svog obilja: lit. 'out of the horn of its abundance'.

napojiti: we have no transitive verb in English relating to drink, to correspond to 'to feed', except 'to water' (of cattle). *Sve* ('everybody') is the object of *napoji*.

... *se kune:* 'vows' (infin. *kleti se*).

anđelima: nom. sing. *anđeo*.

uzorno: the adjective *uzoran* means 'exemplary'. No single adverb in English quite covers this meaning; *uzor*, 'model', 'example'.

osoblje: neut. sing. collective. TYS-Cr pp. 140–1.
osoba: 'a person', is fem. in form, though it may be masc. or fem. in meaning.

p. 82 MIROSLAV KRLEŽA (b. 1893), a Croat, is a prominent personality in 20th century Yugoslav literature, an outstanding writer in every field. A short extract from one of his earlier essays, *O Kranjčevićevoj lirici* (1932), typical of his powerful style, has been included in this book without a translation, as a challenge to those who have read so far.

O KRANJČEVIĆEVOJ LIRICI

Kranjčević: Silvije Strahimir Kranjčević, Croatian poet (1865–1908).

pred konac: 'just before the end'. TYS-Cr p. 184.

pomodan: 'fashionable'.

faktura: French *facture*, here meaning literary composition and style.

retuš: French *retouche*, the 'touching-up'. Such loan words are typical of Krleža's rich vocabulary; where their meaning is obvious no explanatory note is given here.

poslastičar: 'confectioner'.

caklina: lit. 'enamel'; here 'sugar icing'.

osamdesetih godina: 'in the eighties'.

rasvjeta: 'lighting', 'illumination'.

uprljano: 'sullied'.

svladano: 'subdued', 'restrained'.

sudar: 'collision', 'conflict'.

zla: gen. of the noun *zlo*, 'evil'.

rugoba: 'ugliness'.

uokviren: 'framed'.

nadzemaljski: 'super-terrestrial'.

kič: German *Kitsch*, 'trash'.

žanr-drvorezi: 'woodcut-style works', French *genre*, here 'style', 'type'; *drvorez*, 'woodcut', 'wood-engraving'.

'Nada': a literary periodical.

obilato: 'profusely'.

u koje je gledao kao u: 'which he looked to as to'.

književnopomodna: lit. 'literarily-fashionable', a characteristic compound word.

kod svoga izražavanja: lit. 'at his expressing', i.e. 'in expressing himself'.

više odmagalo nego pomagalo: 'more hindered than helped'. Both verbs, *odmagati* and *pomagati* (both ipf.) take the dative case. TYS-Cr p. 179.

smetati: 'to hamper' and *pogodovati*, 'to be favourable to', also both take the dative.

vanjski: 'on the surface'.

vještački: 'artificial'.

naprava: 'device', 'contrivance'.

steznik: 'corsets', 'stays'.

kora: 'outer crust', e.g. bark (of a tree).

prodirati: pres. *prodirem*; 'to penetrate'.

kranjčevićevski: 'characteristic of Kranjčević'; a typical 'coined' adjective.

pojava: 'phenomenon'.

markantan: 'significant'.

Reči su mu po smislu: 'His words are, in their meaning'.

podzemni huk . . . ponornice: 'the subterranean roar of an underground river'.

valjati se: 'to roll'.

istinito: 'truthfully', 'genuinely'.

sudbonosno: 'ominously'.

Bibliography

1 Works represented in this book

(The dates are those of the editions used)

Dragutin Tadijanović: *Pjesme i proza*, 1969.
Tvrtko Čubelić: *Narodne pripovijetke*, 1963.
Antonije Isaković: *Velika deca*, 1958.
Ivan Slamnig: *Neprijatelj*, 1959.
Radomir Konstantinović: *Daj nam danas*, 1963.
Petar Šegedin: *Na putu*, 1963.
Mihajlo Lalić: *Zlo proljeće*, 1953.
Meša Selimović: *Tišine*, 1965.
Nikola Šop: *Tajanstvena prela*, 1943.
Slobodan Novak: *Mirisi, zlato i tamjan*, 1968.
Aleksandar Vučo: *Raspust*, 1954.
Antun Šoljan: *Izdajice*, 1961.
Vladan Desnica: *Proljeća Ivana Galeba*, 1957.
Ranko Marinković: *Kiklop*, 1966.
Miroslav Krleža: *Eseji*, Vol. II, 1963.
Ivo Andrić's short story *Čudo u Olovu*, first published in 1931,
here taken from a 1958 edition, has been reprinted in many
collections, including one by Vera Javarek: *Serbo-Croation
Prose and Verse* (without translations), published in England
in 1955. This also contains a longer extract from Miroslav
Krleža's essay *O Kranjčevićevoj lirici*.
Aleksandar Vučo's novel *Raspust* has been translated by Alec
Brown, with the title *The Holidays* (1959).
The illustrated monthly magazine *Review*, which provided the
material for the short extracts from articles, can be ordered
from the Editor, Terazije 31, Belgrade.

2 Dictionaries, Grammar and Encyclopaedia

The list of Dictionaries is in chronological order, according to
the dates of the most recent editions.

1. F. A. Bogadek: *English–Croatian Croatian–English Dictionary*, 1 volume, 497 pp., Pittsburgh, 1947.
2. R. Filipović and others: *English–Croatian Dictionary*, 1 volume, 1,430 pp., Zagreb, 1955.
3. S. Ristić, Ž. Simić and V. Popović: *English–Serbo-Croat Dictionary*, 2 volumes, Belgrade, 1956. An encyclopaedic dictionary, containing the Serbo-Croatian equivalents of about 100,000 English words and phrases.
4. S. Ristić and Ž. Simić: *Englesko-srpskohrvatski rečnik*, 1 volume, 867 pp., Belgrade, 1959.
5. M. Drvodelić: *Croato-Serbian–English Dictionary*, 1 volume, 912 pp., Zagreb, 1961.
6. B. Grujić: *Englesko-srpskohrvatski školski rečnik*, 1 volume, 599 pp., Titograd, 1966.
7. M. Drvodelić: *English–Croato-Serbian Dictionary*, 1 volume, 1,163 pp., Zagreb, 1970.
8. Morton Benson: *Serbo-Croatian–English Dictionary*, I volume, 807 pp. University of Pennsylvania Press, 1971.

Vera Javarek and Miroslava Sudjić: *Teach Yourself Serbo-Croat*, 2nd Edn., 1972.

Cassell's *Encyclopaedia of World Literature*, 1973, is recommended for biographies of Yugoslav writers.